"As much as we might wish for an easier path to personal growth, the most effective ones often seem to be paved with heartache, despair, and fears that throw us unceremoniously to our knees. Each section of Hibbert's excellent book *Who Am I Without You?* is filled with valuable information, unfailing compassion, and practical healing techniques that can help you move and grow through the brokenness of grief, disillusionment, and fear."

—**Sue Patton Thoele**, author of *The Courage to Be Yourself* and *The Mindful Woman*

"*Who Am I Without You?* is the light at the end of the tunnel! Christina Hibbert has written a compassionate guide for surviving a breakup with a sensitivity and exquisite insight that even in the heartbreak of relationship loss, there is an opportunity for psychological change and personal growth."

—**Diana Lynn Barnes, PsyD**, psychotherapist specializing in women's mental health, coauthor of *The Journey to Parenthood*, and editor and contributing author of *Women's Reproductive Mental Health Across the Lifespan*

"With just the right blend of empathy for the reader's pain and encouragement to move forward, Christina Hibbert has written an accessible, practical, and compassionate guidebook for reclaiming self-worth after a breakup. I've seen hundreds of women in my psychotherapy practice who feel unworthy of love, and whose self-esteem has taken a blow after a failed relationship—and I wish I'd had this book to recommend to them! *Who Am I Without You?* is a much-needed companion on the road to resolving emotional barriers, reclaiming your worth, and re-envisioning a life of love after loss."

—**Julie de Azevedo Hanks, LCSW**, psychotherapist, author of *The Burnout Cure*, and owner and executive director of Wasatch Family Therapy

Who am I without you?

52 Ways to Rebuild Self-Esteem After a Breakup

●—♥—●

Christina G. Hibbert, PsyD

New Harbinger Publications, Inc.

Publisher's Note

Distributed in Canada by Raincoast Books

Copyright © 2015 by Christina G. Hibbert
         New Harbinger Publications, Inc.
         5674 Shattuck Avenue
         Oakland, CA 94609
         www.newharbinger.com

Cover design by Amy Shoup
Interior design by Michele Waters-Kermes
Acquired by Wendy Millstine
Edited by Marisa Solís

Library of Congress Cataloging-in-Publication Data on file

Printed in the United States of America

22   21   20

10   9   8   7   6   5   4   3   2

Contents

Foreword

When I was thirty years old, my first husband became obsessed with a woman in our social circle whom I thought of as a good friend. For months, I used denial to protect myself from facing the reality of their relationship. Eventually, of course, I had to face my fear and acknowledge the truth. The double betrayal of husband and friend was devastating. The thought of my two little boys being the children of divorce, and the idea of being a single parent, was guilt-inducing, terrifying, and incredibly saddening. I did everything I could to save the marriage—each attempt unsuccessful and many at the expense of my own well-being, including "reconciling" three times. Some, rightly, called those my "peace-at-any-price groveling times." However, as the adage goes, "It takes two to make a marriage work;" and a couple of years after learning the truth, I found myself staggering through the wreckage of a failed marriage and the disintegration of life as I knew, and wanted, it.

Yes, the marriage was beyond repair. Worse yet, for a long time, I felt I was too.

If you are in a similar position right now—or have troubling residual feelings from a past breakup—please do yourself a huge favor and allow *Who Am I Without You?* to become your friend and guide. I truly believe the healing and growth that took me years and years to achieve would have taken much less time if I'd had access to the invaluable insights and tools offered in *Who Am I Without You?* Author and psychologist Christina Hibbert divides her book into three main sections: Overcoming, Becoming, and Flourishing. Each is filled with valuable information, unfailing compassion, and practical healing techniques to help you move through the brokenness of grief, disillusionment, and fear. The reader can feel Dr. Hibbert's understanding radiating from the pages and, in the light of that perception and encouragement, is given the opportunity to make steady progress toward healing and wholeness.

As much as we might wish for an easier path to personal growth, the most effective ones often seem to be paved with heartache, despair, and fears that throw us unceremoniously to our knees. While some breakthroughs and enlightenments may come softly, quietly, and in bite-size pieces, mine are more often gleaned from the impetus of pain and loss. Such was the case with my divorce. Even though it took a long time, my story has a happy outcome. My career as a psychotherapist evolved from the pain and insights of that journey, and my first book, *The Courage to Be Yourself,* was inspired by the commitment to self-love and acceptance I uncovered while sifting through the shards of my pre- and postdivorce lack of self-worth. Best of all, this year, the love of my life and I will celebrate our fortieth wedding anniversary.

Upon looking back on extremely painful experiences, people often comment, "It was really the best thing that ever happened to me." I definitely can say that of my divorce. If you are going through the fire of a breakup now, I hope eventually you will feel the same way. With the help of *Who Am I Without You?,* I'm sure you will.

—Sue Patton Thoele
Author of *The Courage to Be Yourself* and
The Mindful Woman, among others

Introduction

You're most likely picking up this book because you're going through a hard time—because a relationship has been broken, and now you feel broken, too. Maybe you've just ended a ten-year relationship. Maybe you're experiencing your first heartache. Either way, you have come to the right place.

I know how it is to feel broken—your heart so heavy in your chest you fear you'll never breathe freely again. I also know how it is to wake up one day to find that you're not only put back together, you're better than before. This book is a guide for women of all ages experiencing all levels of heartache. I've written it with the exact words and tools I've used to help my friends, family, and clients through their breakups, divorces, and other life transitions.

These pages also include the methods I have used in my times of brokenness. That's what this book is about: helping you break through the pain of your breakup so that you may discover healing, and showing you the way to lifelong self-esteem and joy.

Why Focus on Self-Esteem?

This book isn't like every other breakup book. It has a unique focus: self-esteem. Your self-esteem can be crushed after a breakup, but the good news is that it's repairable.

"Self-esteem" means how we feel about ourselves—not only when things are right but when things are *not* right. It determines how we rise after we fall and how we put the pieces back together after we've been broken. Self-*esteem*—what we think, believe, and feel about ourselves—is based on self-*worth*, who we really are. We must understand who we truly are—to see the good, bad, ugly, *and* exceptional—and embrace it if we want to feel self-worth and experience unwavering self-esteem.

It *is* possible to discover your worth, even if it *feels* impossible now. It *is* possible for that discovery to lead to healthier relationships down the road. Your self-esteem will increase and you'll enjoy all the benefits of living a life of confidence, hope, and, yes, love.

How This Book Is Set Up

Years ago, in my clinical psychology practice, I learned that if I only focused on helping clients *overcome* their struggles, I was doing them a disservice. We need to build on the positives just as much, or even more, than we need to rid ourselves of the negatives. That's when I came up with my professional focus and tagline: Overcoming. Becoming. Flourishing.

Overcoming. Becoming. Flourishing.

Each of us is either *overcoming* something, working on *becoming* the best we can be, or seeking the finest of life—*flourishing*. Chances are, if you're fresh from a breakup, you're reading this book because you're back to square one: overcoming. But you mustn't sell yourself short and settle for *only* overcoming. That's why this book is written in three parts: *Overcoming* Brokenness, Building Unwavering

Self-Esteem (or *becoming*), and Learning to Love and Be Loved Again (or *flourishing*). Yes, if you stick with me, you will overcome, become, *and* flourish!

52 Short, Sweet Chapters

You may have noticed that there are fifty-two chapters. That's to remind you that self-esteem after a breakup takes time—sometimes a few weeks, sometimes a few months, sometimes a year, sometimes longer. Give yourself the time you need to do the work in this book, and feel free to work through chapters in the order that's best for you.

Tools for Rebuilding

Each chapter ends with several tools, or exercises. I encourage you to do them all. These are the how-tos of the principles discussed in each chapter—the tools that will help you fix what feels broken.

Many of the tools require you to write things down, so designate a notebook or journal (paper or digital) specifically for these exercises. Most will also require continued practice long after you've finished this book. At least, that's what I hope you'll do—continue to practice. Learning and implementing these tools will make the difference between merely *understanding* the ideas and using this book to make change and *grow*.

Don't Give Up!

Bottom line: You're going to your have ups and downs. That's part of overcoming a breakup, and that's part of developing unwavering self-esteem and learning to love again. The trick is to get back *up* after every "down." Use this book as a counselor, motivator, teacher, and friend. Do the exercises, and use the tools. Then get out there: Overcome. Become. Flourish!

PART 1

Overcoming Brokenness
How to Cope, Grieve, and Come out Stronger on the Other Side

1 You're not alone.

I think this is what we all want to hear: that
we are not alone in hitting the bottom, and
that it is possible to come out of that place
courageous, beautiful, and strong.

—Anna White

Relationship loss—we've all experienced it or will at some point. I'm no exception. I may not have experienced your exact heartache or circumstances, but trust me: I understand loss. I'm here to help you through it.

Knowing you're not alone is incredibly important when a relationship ends, because it can *feel* very alone. You might find yourself saying, "No one gets how I feel right now." You're right: No one can understand *exactly* how you feel. We each have our unique experience of loss after a breakup. However, it's also true that you may be feeling many of the same things women have been feeling for years—and recognizing what you have in common can actually be freeing.

If You Feel Broken from Your Breakup, You're Not Alone

Experiencing a breakup is a universal loss. The sad truth is that breakups and divorce are one of the most common human experiences. Just look at the statistics:

- 40 to 50 percent of marriages end in divorce in the United States (APA 2013).

- For second marriages, the divorce rate is 60 to 65 percent, and for third marriages it's 72 to 74 percent (Divorce Statistics 2013).

- Though there aren't any solid statistics on breakups, the general consensus is that one-third of women have experienced a significant breakup in the past ten years.

Whether you're young or old, divorcing or splitting from your boyfriend, whether it ended civilly or with a text that read, "Sorry, babe. It's over," *it still hurts.* Considering these statistics, there are a lot of hurting women out there.

You're *not* alone.

If Your Self-Esteem Has Taken a Hit After Your Breakup, You're Not Alone

How is your self-esteem right now? If you're fresh from a breakup, I would guess it's at an all-time low. Take this brief assessment and see for yourself.

Self-Esteem Assessment

Directions

Place a checkmark beside all sentences that apply to you right now.

1. I feel confident most of the time. _____

2. I often think negatively about myself. ✓_____

3. I feel worthy of love. _____

4. I am fearful of or sensitive to rejection. ✓_____

5. I accept my flaws and work on them. ✓_____

6. I give others' opinions of me more weight than my own. __✓___

7. I take good care of myself and tend to my needs. _____

8. I often compare myself, my life, or my relationships to others. ✓___

9. I feel attractive. _____

10. I feel that other people don't accept me. _____

11. I feel capable of achieving success in my life. _____

12. I often feel fearful or anxious, especially around others. _✓____

13. I often think positively about myself. _____

14. I feel inadequate or inferior to others. __✓___

15. I embrace my strengths *and* my weaknesses. _____

16. I am concerned, and often critical, about my body and looks. _✓___

17. I feel comfortable in social situations. __✓___

18. I have difficulty trusting others. _✓____

19. I understand who I really am, and I like me. _____

20. I am a perfectionist. _____

Scoring

Give yourself 1 point for every odd number you checked, and 1 point for every even number you *did not* check. Add up your score. Then find your score among the categories below.

Results

16–20: High Self-Esteem
Your self-esteem seems strong, especially considering all you've been going through. This doesn't mean that you don't have a thing or two to learn about self-worth and self-esteem, but it does mean you're starting off in pretty great shape.

11–15: High Average Self-Esteem
You have your moments when you feel "less than," but overall your self-esteem is okay. There's room for improvement, but you've got a foundation on which to build.

6–10: Low Average Self-Esteem
You struggle with self-esteem, or, at least, you're struggling now. Don't worry, though. That's what this book is for: to show you how to improve.

0–5: Low Self-Esteem ← *ugh!*
Your self-esteem has definitely taken a hit—either from your breakup or from earlier in life. You're not the only one who struggles, however, and you're certainly not beyond hope. Together, we will help you discover the truth about who you are and rebuild your sense of self-worth.

Did I Mention That You're Not Alone?

I'm here. Or rather, this book is here—with my words, encouragement, comfort, motivation, direction, and, yes, love. You can open this book anytime and know that as I write these words for you I do so out of respect and admiration for your willingness to work through your heartache. I do so out of a desire for you to know you're not alone. One day, you'll be *flourishing* in life and love again.

Bottom Line...

- Yep, you guessed it! *You're not alone.* And don't you forget it.

Tool: Examine Your True Feelings

- ♥ When I say, "You're not alone," how do you feel? Do you believe me? Do you have doubts? Write about this in your journal or notebook. *It lands hollow right now I feel very alone*

- ♥ How do you feel about your self-esteem assessment score? In what ways might your self-esteem be impacted by your breakup? Did you struggle with self-esteem previously? Can you relate to any of the things I've written in this chapter, like feeling "less than" or "unlovable"? Why or why not? Write it down.

my self esteem is super low. I knew it would be — I've always struggled with it. On one level I know I'm capable and competent. But I keep screwing things up. It's way too easy for me to feel rejected. I have been looking for love — self love, self acceptance from outside myself. I don't know how to love myself. That puts too much on others — then on some level I think I feel upset when of course — they can't give that to me

2 Set up your support system.

Alone we can do so little; together we can do so much.

—Helen Keller

I'm not the only one who's here. Your support system is also here for you, even if it's not yet assembled. Getting through a breakup *requires* support. Like scaffolding around a newly constructed building, your friends, family, and community can surround and sustain you as you put yourself back together and grow.

Set Up Your Scaffolding

"Can you tell me about your support system?" It's one of my first questions for clients experiencing a breakup, loss, or crisis. Some can answer easily, "I have a great support system—my mom, sister, best friend, and church members." Others respond, "I don't have a clue where I can turn for support." No matter your situation, if you want to stay afloat you're going to need support. If you don't feel like you already have one, a solid support system can be created, though it might take some effort. Of course, family and friends should be part of your support system, but if that's not a viable option for you, then reach out to coworkers, neighbors, community service providers, or your faith community. Don't give up. Keep seeking until you find the support you need.

There are different ways your family, friends, and community can support you through your breakup, including:

- **Practical support.** Let others bring you meals or take you out once in a while. Let them help with housework, errands, or, if you have kids, childcare.

- **Emotional support.** Let others listen as you talk, cry, and process what you're feeling. Let them be there to strengthen you as you set boundaries with your ex, work through emotions, and rediscover your self-worth.

- **Informational support.** Let those with professional expertise inform, advise, or counsel you as needed. This may include psychological, medical, legal, financial, or ecclesiastical support.

Let Yourself Be Supported...for Now

If you're like many women, you may be thinking, "I don't need help from others. I can do this on my own." Why do we women have such a hard time accepting help?

Some of us might believe asking for or accepting help makes us weak, but it doesn't. It isn't weak to need others. On the contrary, relying upon others for support makes you stronger, for you're no longer trying to do it all by yourself. We all need each other, and for now, you need help, so use it.

Tips for Asking for and Receiving Help

Use these four steps to get the help you need.

1. **Before you can *ask* for what you need, you have to *know* what you need.** Ask yourself, "What do I need—physically,

emotionally, intellectually, socially, and spiritually—right now?" Ask often. *just a few consistent people I can connect with & share what I'm feeling maybe get advice*

2. **Once you know what you need, state it clearly.** People are not mind readers. Stating clearly what you need is crucial to actually getting it. Say, "I need to talk with someone about my breakup—*today*." Say, "All you need to do is listen and be there." Be clear. Be direct. Be willing to ask for *exactly* what you need.

3. **Ask the right person.** If you need help with child care, ask someone who loves your child; if you need someone to listen, ask someone who can let you be the focus of the conversation for a while. Keep asking until you find the person who is willing and able to serve you best.

4. **Don't forget to ask your Higher Power.** Divine support may come in the form of words from a friend, a dream, or a song that speaks to your soul. It may be a feeling of peace that sweeps over you or a sudden knowing of what you must do. However it comes, connect to the Source that knows and understands your needs better than anyone. It's the surest way to receive exactly what you need.

Bottom Line...

- We all need support in times of distress.

- Asking for and receiving help from your support system makes you stronger.

Tool: Set Up Your Support System and Utilize It

♥   Brainstorm a list of people and places to turn to for help. This might include friends, parents, siblings, adult children, coworkers, clergymen, community resources, online groups or forums, or professional services like counseling, massage, medical support, et cetera. List each support person on the left side of your journal. On the right side, write specifically what she or he can do.

♥   Select one person from your list who can help you fulfill a need you have *right now*. Reach out to that person *today*.

Sundance
Andrew Byce
John Ribera
Bob's
Steere R

3 Help others help you.

Many times a wedge is driven between those suffering
the loss and very dear and close friends. We can refer
to this as a "wedge of ignorance"—ignorance about the
great importance of open and physical communication."

—Ronald J. Knapp

As hard as you work to gather support, at times it may feel as if no one really gets it. It's easy for people to misunderstand loss of any kind, especially the loss of a relationship. Friends and family might say the wrong thing or might not say anything, which can leave you feeling like no one takes your loss seriously. But don't give up. You can educate, illuminate, and help your loved ones help *you*.

Grief Can Change Relationships

Seeking support when you're experiencing grief over a breakup can be a challenge. Family members may not be available, due to their own life circumstances or their relationship to you and your ex. Friends may not understand; they may be too busy with their own life stress or may just not know how to be there for you. Many who have experienced loss, including from breakups, say that their circle of friends changed significantly. We may filter out friends or family members who seem emotionally insensitive, who lack depth or perspective, or who were simply absent in our time of need.

Sometimes professional counseling is the only place to turn. It's essential that the person you're working with, however, is familiar with relationship loss and grief work, that he or she can handle your grief, and that he or she not try and force you to be somewhere you're not. Keep trying until you find the support that is right for you.

Misperceptions About Grief After a Breakup

Under the cloud of grief after a breakup, it's almost impossible to see anything but the pain you're feeling. So many good intentions fall by the wayside as family and friends try to "be there" for you, only to push you farther away. Most people actually have no idea how to handle grief. They try to be there for those they love but often end up driving a wedge instead. Grief-stricken, we may end up feeling isolated, judged, misunderstood, or alone.

Here are some of the common misperceptions of grief that get in our way:

- **The need to "say something."** When someone has just experienced a major loss, there is usually nothing that can or needs to be said. The important thing is to be there.

- **Trite reassurances are supportive.** *Overused sayings meant to be encouraging* such as, "You're better off now," or "Time heals all wounds," though well meant, are better left unsaid.

- **Support people must share their own experiences of loss.** When well-meaning friends and family overshare their stories of loss, it can minimize your experience. Hearing, "I know *exactly* how you feel," or "I understand completely," can isolate us further, as we come to feel our problems are generic and unimportant.

Ways to Support Someone Through Grief

So what are some of the best ways for others to support you after your breakup? They can:

1. Just be there.

2. Listen.

3. Let you talk and cry, and talk and cry, without putting a time limit on it and without judgment.

4. Allow you to tell your story as often as you need.

5. Encourage expression of the facts, details, and emotions related to the breakup.

6. Check in on you. They can say, "I'm just calling to see how you're doing today." No pressure or expectations.

7. When they feel the urge to say something trite to you, like, "This too shall pass," they should hold their tongue. Instead, they should say, "I'm so sorry," let you cry, and cry with you.

It's good to ask for these things from those who are trying to support you. In fact, you may want to read this list off to your support people, or just copy this chapter and pass it along.

Bottom Line...

- Most of us need to be taught how to support others through the grief of a breakup.

- Avoiding the mistakes and doing the right thing is as simple as reading this chapter, implementing its suggestions, and passing them on.

Tool: How to Feel Understood

♥ What do you wish others would understand about or say to you? Write about it in your journal. Communicate it to your support system.

♥ Apply the ideas listed in Ways to Support Someone Through Grief to *yourself.*

♥ Consider counseling to process grief and emotions related to your breakup if you need additional help.

4. Set healthy boundaries.

All of our unhappiness comes from
our inability to be alone.

—Jean de la Bruyere

In chapters 1 and 2, I emphasized, "You're not alone" and "You need support." Now I'm saying, "Set up boundaries." It sounds inconsistent, but you need time away from unhealthy relationships—to get clear, to grieve, and to rediscover who you really are. You cannot overcome, become, and flourish if you're still seesawing with your ex. You need to set some boundaries.

Why Boundaries?

"Setting boundaries" is just psychobabble for establishing healthy rules and guidelines in a relationship. Without boundaries, relationships cannot thrive. For instance, think of a mother and child. If the mother has no boundaries with her child—that is, no system of rules, discipline, instruction, and respect—the child will never learn important life and social skills. The same goes for friendships and intimate relationships. Boundaries keep both parties safe. They keep our interactions healthy and productive.

Setting Boundaries Is Hard!

"I feel mean setting boundaries," "I'm just not good at it," or "I keep trying, but it never seems to work." I hear these things all the time. Boundary setting isn't easy, and it can be especially tough to set boundaries with an ex. You're used to being part of one another's lives, and it's common to struggle with this at first. However, if you stick with the boundaries you set, you will find a much healthier situation for both you and your ex.

If You Don't Set Boundaries...

Here are three reasons why it's crucial to set and keep boundaries:

1. Getting back together, on and off, almost always prolongs the inevitable and causes more pain.

2. Keeping constant contact—either verbally or physically—prevents both of you from grieving and moving forward.

3. You cannot truly move on if an ex is still influencing you. Making a clean break is especially important in cases where your ex has been extremely controlling.

How Do I Set Boundaries?

The following suggestions can be used to set healthy boundaries with your ex and any other unhealthy relationships. You can always redefine your boundaries later, if you wish, but for now, you need space and safety to get through this breakup.

- **Decide how much contact you will or won't have with your ex.** Ask yourself, "How much contact is healthy for me right now? Do I need to limit in-person contact? Phone calls? Texting?" Be realistic but firm. If you have children together, for instance, or are going through legal proceedings such as a divorce, you may have to see your ex more often than you'd like. That doesn't mean you can't still set boundaries.

- **Decide how you will or won't let your ex treat you.** Anticipate how it will go if you do have contact with your ex. What behavior is okay? What behavior is not? Does he try to push your boundaries? If so, what does he do, and how can you prevent it?

- **Write your boundaries down in plain, clear terms.** Then put them on your fridge or bathroom mirror—somewhere they'll be easy to see. They'll remind you of your goal—a healthy relationship—in times when it feels tough.

- **Clearly communicate your boundaries to your ex.** Write him a letter or email, or give him a copy of the boundaries you wrote down and posted. If you talk in person, be firm and clear. For example, "I cannot see or talk with you right now. I can only reply to text messages, and only about _____." Fill in the blank with whatever is vital at that moment, like "selling our house."

- **Remember that boundaries are not there to punish someone else.** They are there to keep *you* safe and healthy.

- **Don't confuse being needed with being loved.** When someone loves you, he or she respects your boundaries.

- **Prioritize your needs right now.** Your goal is to heal from this breakup and rediscover your self-worth. That's an important need. Don't let your ex stand in your way.

Maintaining a Healthy Relationship with Your Ex

If you choose to do so—and when the time is right and you're ready—it *is* possible to have a healthy relationship with your ex. Just make sure to…

- **Allow time to heal.** After the breakup, give both of you time to heal before you try to figure out your new relationship.

- **Work on building your self-worth separately from him.** Encourage him to do the same. Then you'll both be ready for a healthy friendship.

- **Practice forgiveness when you're ready.** Ask him to forgive you, too. (More on forgiveness in chapter 36.)

- **Redefine your relationship.** Now that you're not "together," you need to agree on what your relationship will be. For example, you could agree to work together as "coparents," or to keep a respectful friendship. Whatever it will be, make sure you discuss and work it out together.

- **If needed, reestablish boundaries.** If your newly defined relationship ever starts feeling controlling or unhealthy, go back and reestablish the boundaries you set before.

Bottom Line…

- You need time away from your ex—for now.

- Healthy relationships, by definition, have healthy boundaries. And healthy boundaries will allow you to move forward in your healing and personal growth.

Tool: Set Healthy Boundaries

- ♥ Using the suggestions in this chapter, set boundaries with your ex.

- ♥ Call upon your support system to help you decide which boundaries need to be set and how to best communicate them to your ex. Then rely upon your support people to keep you strong as you enforce them.

5 Put yourself on your list.

Love yourself first, and everything else
falls in line. You really have to love
yourself to get anything done in this world.

—Lucille Ball

We women are fabulous at taking care of others, at getting our to-do lists done. But are *you* on your list? Too often we put our needs last or forget them altogether. You can't afford to forget yourself right now. Let's put you back on your list and get this important job done right.

You're Not Selfish

Many of us confuse "self-care" with "self-*ish*." Allow me to set it straight: *It is not selfish to take care of yourself*. Disregarding self-care is like a mother who says she loves her kids, then doesn't feed them. It's ultimately more selfish *not* to practice self-care, for we burn out and then can't care for others. Self-care is crucial to self-esteem and self-love. It's especially important during hard times, like after a valued relationship ends. If we don't take care of ourselves, we simply will not have the endurance to overcome, become, or flourish.

The Three Layers of Self-Care

I believe there are three layers of self-care: Absolute-Necessity Self-Care, Essential Self-Care, and Icing-on-the-Cake Self-Care.

Absolute-Necessity Self-Care

This base layer of self-care involves doing those things that are absolutely necessary for your health and wellness. Absolute-necessity self-care includes things like getting enough sleep, eating right, and exercising—the basics. Your absolute-necessity needs may change day to day. Some days you absolutely need to get out of the house, other times you need a nap. Without this foundational layer of self-care, you will eventually burn out. Focus first on the absolute necessities to keep yourself strong and well, and you will be more effective as you work through your breakup.

Essential Self-Care

Layer two involves making time for things that are important but might not be absolutely necessary, or even possible, every day. These things are essential in maintaining your physical, emotional, mental, social, and spiritual strength, and may include things such as: time to process, learn, and grow; time to focus on understanding what you're going through; and forming healthy connections with others. Though we don't always believe it, it *is* essential to create space for the activities and people who continually remind us of who we are. If you reach layer two self-care, you will find greater energy, hope, and light in your life.

Icing-on-the-Cake Self-Care

The top layer of self-care involves those things that you might not always get to do but that definitely make you happy when they come around. Things like attending a concert, traveling, playing sports, a special evening on the town with friends, or enjoying the sunset from a hammock are just some ways to give yourself extra TLC. You might not feel much like having fun, relaxing, or playing, but it's important to make time for these things, especially when you're in the midst of heartache. You don't have to go out and have fun *all* the time, but you do need *some* play in your life. In fact, research shows that play is essential to greater happiness and life satisfaction (B. Brown 2012). Look for and create opportunities to take a break from the pain, to have a little fun, to laugh and be with people who really care about you. It will be your icing on the cake.

Bottom Line...

- Right now *you* need to be on your list.

- Self-care is essential to rediscover the deeper, higher, truer aspects of who you are.

Tool: Practice Self-Care

- ♥ Are *you* on your to-do list? If not, add yourself today. It doesn't need to be a grand gesture or take long; it can even involve friends or family—but do something now.

- ♥ How are you doing as caretaker of your self? Ask the following questions: "What do I need?" "What do I want?" "What do I crave?" Based on these things, list your Absolute-Necessity, Essential, and Icing-on-the-cake Self-Care plan. Write how you will implement your plan, then get to work.

6 Accept what is.

Being entirely honest with oneself is a good exercise.

—Sigmund Freud

A huge part of overcoming and moving on after a breakup is accepting where you currently are. It's harder to do than it sounds. We wish we could be in the past, when things were good and our relationship was strong. Or we wish we could be in the future, feeling happy, or in a new, thriving relationship.

We only have the present, however. The past is behind us, and the future will arrive present moment by present moment. It can certainly be challenging, but accepting where you are—what has happened, and how you feel about it—is part of moving forward. In fact, it is the *only* way forward.

Accepting What Is Helps You Move On

Without accepting what *is*, we stay stuck. Emma had recently broken up with her boyfriend of five years when she showed up in my office seeking help for what she called "depression." As we discussed her symptoms, however, it was clear that she was actually in the throes of grief over her breakup. She explained that her boyfriend had dumped her nearly three months ago, but she said she was over it. The more she spoke, the less I believed her story. She wasn't over it. She'd simply shoved the pain away.

Over time, I was able to help Emma see that she hadn't accepted her breakup. Even though on the outside she'd made it seem like she was fine, really, she was fighting the truth. She could not accept how her relationship had ended. She couldn't deal with the pain, so she had tried to escape her present and move on to the future. Yet, there she was—heartbroken and grief-stricken, in my office.

How to Accept What Is

How do we accept what is? Understanding the following is a good place to start.

- **Acceptance doesn't mean you like where you are or that you want to stay there.** Many people confuse "acceptance" with agreement or enjoyment. You don't have to enjoy how you're feeling or agree with how you've been treated. No. You simply have to accept that it *is* the way it is.

- **Acceptance means you're no longer willing to fight with yourself over reality.** You are where you are, and you feel what you feel. You've been through what you've been through. Too often, we fight where we are—wishing, hoping, pushing to be somewhere else—but that's not possible. Instead of *fighting* what has happened, *accept* it.

- **Accepting what is brings peace.** It doesn't automatically make you stop feeling sad or angry or hurt. Accepting what is simply takes away the fight. It frees you from the struggle and, eventually, helps you move on.

- **Acceptance is the first step in overcoming the brokenness.** Once you accept what has happened, you can begin to see all of the broken pieces, and that allows you to, eventually, put them back together.

Bottom Line...

- Give up the fight and accept what *is*.

- You don't have to like it or want it; you just have to accept it.

Tool: Accept What Is

- ❤ Identify those things over which you're fighting yourself. Ask yourself, "Can I accept this?" If not, ask, "What is holding me back?" Ask, "What would my life be like if I simply accepted this breakup and the way things are right now?" Then imagine it and write it down.

- ❤ Take a deep breath, and repeat, "I accept what *is*." Repeat as often as necessary until you actually believe it.

7 Now let it out—FEEL.

Feel, he told himself, feel, feel, feel. Even if what you feel is pain, only let yourself feel.

—P. D. James

I know. It hurts. But running from, ignoring, or denying emotions won't protect you from the pain—not for long, anyway. Now that you're supported and cared for, it's time to *FEEL: Freely Experience Emotions with Love* (Hibbert 2013).

Let Yourself FEEL

You may feel one thing one minute and something completely different the next. That is part of loss and heartache, part of a breakup. The important thing is to let yourself feel whatever emotion comes. Common emotions include: sadness, pain, anxiety, stress, grief, fear, anger, and also insecurity, guilt, or even shame.

Powerful emotions can be scary. We fear feeling them because we believe they will overtake us. Grief, anger, sadness, pain, and fear can feel intense and overwhelming. So we ignore, distract ourselves from, and eventually box these emotions up and shove them deep down in an effort to prevent the frightening consequences we envision if they were ever to escape. The longer feelings are buried, however, the more they fester and grow, until *they* control *us*, stronger than ever.

Emotions Are Simply Emotions

Emotions can feel immense, but what are we really afraid of? I myself have experienced being gripped by emotion many times, believing it is my entire reality—only to eventually see the truth again, that my feelings are simply *feelings*. They have many origins, including my circumstances, health, and how tired I am. Yet I have the power to overcome my emotions.

I now think of emotions as being "like the clouds that float across the sky, which never stay for long. Though they appear threatening, the most they can do is rain or hail or snow for a little while. In raining, hailing, snowing, the clouds lose their power. They literally dissipate" (Hibbert 2013, 183). Feelings, once felt, don't usually linger.

How to FEEL

Instead of running from, ignoring, burying, or fearing emotions, we need to *Freely Experience Emotion with Love*. It's not easy, especially if you're used to ignoring feelings, but don't forget that it *is* possible—and it's one of the best ways to get through the emotions.

Don't force it. Simply feel what is there. You can do this on your own or utilize your support system. These suggestions might help:

- **When you're heartbroken, feel sad and cry.** Talk or write about it. Sit with the feeling as long as you can, taking breaks as needed and repeating until the emotions lighten. You can apply this strategy to any emotion, including anger or anxiety. Remember: the feelings are not you, they are just emotions.

- **Don't forget the last part of FEEL: Love.** Show yourself love as you FEEL. Have compassion for yourself. Give yourself the gift of a soothing bath or a night out with your girlfriends. It's hard to FEEL, so reward yourself when you do.

Bottom Line...

- The only way to heal from intense emotions is to FEEL them: Freely Experience Emotions with Love.

- Use your support system as needed or do it on your own, but the next time a powerful emotion comes, sit still, breathe, and practice FEELing (see below).

Tool: Practice FEELing

♥ Sit in a quiet, calm place. Inhale deeply, pulling the breath from your toes up through your body. Exhale slowly, forcing all the air out of your body, for a count of ten. Repeat five times. Then breathe regularly, and as an emotion arises let it come. Imagine the emotion occurring right in front of you as you lean away. Can you feel how this emotion is not *you*? Ask yourself, "What is this emotion trying to teach me? What can I learn?"

♥ If needed, set a timer for FEELing. Even ten or fifteen minutes can help lighten the load. Repeat each day, decreasing time as appropriate.

8 Worry: It's good for nothing.

> Worry does not empty tomorrow of its sorrow.
> It empties today of its strength.
>
> **—Corrie ten Boom**

Feeling worried is only natural when your relationship ends. Thoughts like, "What's going to happen to me now?" "I'll never find love again," and "My life is over," pop up easily after a breakup—and that's okay. They're just thoughts. What's not okay is letting worry control you. Worry is good for nothing. It hijacks your mind and only brings you down.

Worry Is Like Gasoline

If you were to fill can after can with gasoline and pile them in your garage, eventually you'd be in trouble. One little match and *boom*—the whole place would blow. Gasoline isn't meant to be piled and stored, and neither is worry.

If, however, you use gasoline in the tank of your car to help you get somewhere, it's helpful. Worry is the same—it's pointless, and even harmful, unless you use the worry to motivate you into action.

The Worry Tree

How do we handle worry? I've developed a simple yet powerful tool I call the Worry Tree. It can help you stop the worry for good.

Here's how it works:

1. ISSUE CAUSING WORRY: Ask yourself, "Is there anything I can do about this?"

2. NO: If the answer is no, then stop piling up cans of gasoline. Instead, try one of the suggestions in Tips for Vanishing Worry to stop the worry.

3. YES: If the answer is yes, then ask, "Can I do anything about it *now*?"

4. NO: If the answer is no, then you must work to push the worry aside until the time comes when you *can* do something about it.

5. YES: If the answer is "Yes, I can do something right now," then do it!

It sounds simple, and it is—in theory. Often putting off the thing we need to do, like visiting with an attorney about the divorce, cleaning out your ex's stuff, or making a tough phone call, is the *reason* for the worry. When we take care of the thing we don't want but *need* to do, the worry dissipates.

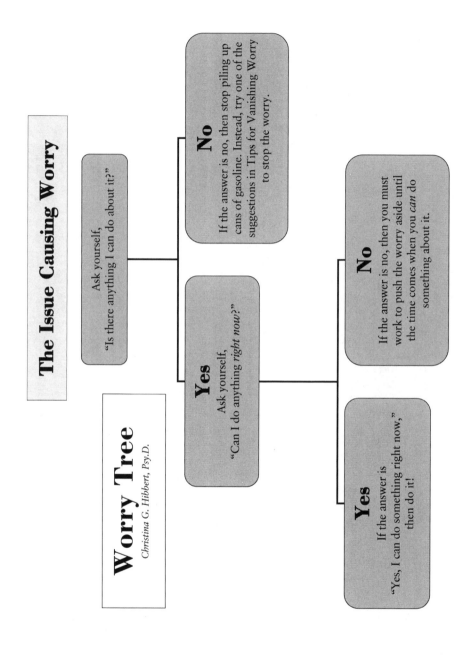

Worry Tree
Christina G. Hibbert, Psy.D.

The Issue Causing Worry

Ask yourself,
"Is there anything I can do about it?"

No
If the answer is no, then stop piling up cans of gasoline. Instead, try one of the suggestions in Tips for Vanishing Worry to stop the worry.

Yes
Ask yourself,
"Can I do anything *right now*?"

No
If the answer is no, then you must work to push the worry aside until the time comes when you *can* do something about it.

Yes
If the answer is
"Yes, I can do something right now," then do it!

Tips for Vanishing Worry

Try these four suggestions to ease your worries.

1. **Distract yourself.** If you can't do anything about the source of the worry right now, then do something to take your mind off it. Choose a healthy distraction, like time with friends, a walk, or reading. Unhealthy distractions—like abusing alcohol or drugs, promiscuous sex, or overeating—will only make things worse in the long run.

2. **Write it out.** Writing is cathartic, especially for worried thinking. Write all your worries down at the top of the page, then write how you feel as you work through the steps of the Worry Tree. Journal about how it feels for worry to control your body and mind, and what you plan to do to take back the control. Get it out of you and onto the page. Then let it go. You can revisit it later if you'd like—it's all there. Or you can burn the paper (or delete your entry) instead!

3. **Call and talk to a friend or family member who can remind you of the truth.** Most worry comes because we blow things out of proportion, forgetting the reality of the situation. If you have a friend who can remind you that "It's going to be okay," sometimes it *does* make everything okay.

4. **Set a "worry date" with yourself.** Set a time and a time limit during which you will focus 100 percent on your worries. Make sure you save all the worrying for your worry date. After a few dates, you'll probably want to break up with your worries.

Note: If your worry becomes intense or feels out of control, you may be experiencing an anxiety disorder. Seeking treatment from a qualified medical or mental health provider can help you manage the worry or anxiety and bring you back to health.

Bottom Line...

- Worry is a natural part of getting through a breakup, but you don't have to get stuck in it.

- You can develop the skills to challenge worry, helping it vanish and giving yourself the much-needed break you deserve.

Tool: Use the Worry Tree to Become Worry-Free

- ♥ List your worries. One by one, select a worry and use the Worry Tree to either take action or let go.

- ♥ Use the Tips for Vanishing Worry to erase any worries that try to stick around.

9 Don't let anger get the best of you.

Anger is an acid that can do more harm to
the vessel in which it is stored than to
anything on which it is poured.

—Mark Twain

Anger is a natural emotion, especially when it comes to the loss of a relationship. You might feel angry about the way things ended—angry about how your ex behaved (or didn't behave), or even angry with yourself for the way things went down. Anger is also a common emotion in loss; you may feel angry that your relationship had to end at all.

Anger is a difficult emotion for many of us, especially women, and one that is also heavily tied to our self-esteem. None of us wants to be "an angry person," so we stuff our anger, never giving it a proper voice, and it ends up coming out when we least expect it, causing trouble and making us feel down about ourselves. We can learn to manage feelings of anger, however, giving us peace of mind and allowing us to take back control.

The Truth About Anger

Understanding the truth about anger can help us better manage our feelings of anger. Here are some things that are helpful to know.

- **Anger is just like any other emotion; it is neither inherently good nor bad.** Just like with other emotions—sadness, fear, or even happiness—it's how we *express* these emotions that can be "good" or "bad," or rather, "helpful" or "unhelpful." Think about it. Even happiness, when expressed gloatingly, can become unhelpful.

- **Anger is a *secondary* emotion.** This means anger usually results from a *primary* emotion—most likely fear, sadness, grief, or pain. Tapping in to the primary emotion can help you work through the anger, instead of letting anger work through *you*. Ask yourself, "What is beneath this anger?" "What is feeding it?" You may be feeling sad about losing the relationship, or perhaps you're afraid of being on your own. A therapist, friend, or family member can help you discover what's underlying the anger. Then, you can FEEL that primary emotion—grieving your loss, for instance—instead of displacing feelings of anger onto some poor, unsuspecting soul.

- **Learning to cope with and express anger in healthy and positive ways is essential to self-esteem.** Managing our emotions helps us feel true to who we really are and how we really want to be.

Expressing Anger: Assertiveness vs. Aggression

There's a difference between using the emotion of anger to be *assertive* and using it to be *aggressive*. Expressing anger assertively, or in ways that calm us down, helps. Assertiveness is saying what needs to be said, doing what must be done. It is taking care of *you*, even if it feels hard to do. In doing that thing which must be done, you become less tense, because you're taking care of yourself and not letting anger get the best of you.

Aggression, on the other hand, is exploding out, escalating, creating more anger—in you and others. It's what gets us worked up and leads to violence, pain, and suffering.

How to Manage Anger

It's the stuffing of anger that causes the most problems. Remember the gasoline we discussed in chapter 8? The same metaphor applies here. Instead of storing anger, you must let yourself *FEEL* and deal with the emotion of anger when it comes.

In addition to the ideas mentioned earlier, here are a few more ways to cope with anger:

- **Write furiously about all the things that are making you fume.** Read it out loud to a trustworthy friend, tear the paper up, or delete the file when you're done.

- **Get out and go for a walk, jog, or any activity that gets you moving.** Anger is an emotion of *action*, so it helps to put your body to good use. (I find kickboxing especially helpful in times of anger!)

- **Talk it out with a trusted friend, family member, or therapist.** Find someone who can just listen about your breakup and your ex, and not take offense or try to change your emotions. Then vent it out. You'll be surprised how much better this can make you feel.

- **Scream into a pillow or an empty house.** Letting it go in a safe environment can prevent you from letting it go onto someone else later.

- **Remind yourself that anger is just an emotion and that it's okay to FEEL it, and even express it, in healthy ways.** Keep reminding yourself for as long as it takes.

Bottom Line...

- Anger is just an emotion—it's not you.

- You can take charge and learn from your anger, and you'll feel much better about yourself if you do.

Tool: Get a Handle on Anger

♥ Try this exercise: Write an angry letter to your ex or anyone toward whom you feel anger. Read it out loud to the air or to someone you trust. Sometimes, just writing and reading the letter is enough, and you realize it doesn't need to be mailed. Feel free to destroy it, then do something kind for yourself.

♥ If you feel that you need to mail the letter, rewrite it. State exactly what needs to be said, and remove any low blows or aggressive phrases. When written carefully, letters are a great way to get your point across, because they allow you time to remove the emotion and prevent you from reacting in anger in the moment.

10 Identify your losses.

Grief is the process that allows us to let go of that
which was and be ready for that which is to come.

—Therese A. Rando

You've experienced significant loss, and now you need to grieve.
You've lost your relationship, yes, but it's more than that. You've lost
the life you knew. You've likely lost your identity—who you were and
who you thought you would be. You've probably lost your self-esteem.
In order to heal, each loss must be grieved. And before you can
grieve, you need to identify your losses.

Understanding Loss

Whether a result of breakup or divorce, death, job loss, moving, or
even financial changes, loss is part of life. Loss and grief are universal, something we all experience at one point or another.

Many of us have trouble recognizing loss, however. I've seen it
over and over. Clients show up in my office after a breakup, a big
move, or even after a friendship has ended; they know they're sad or
angry or hurting, but they fail to identify their pain as loss. All major
change, even positive change, involves loss. That's what change is—
giving up or losing something to become something else.

Loss is hard, even if you wanted the relationship to end. Primary losses often carry with them secondary losses, too. For instance, the primary loss of your relationship may include such secondary losses as financial security; friendships you had as a couple; your role and identity as a girlfriend, partner, or wife; and, yes, your self-image or self-esteem.

Other common symbolic losses related to the breakup of a relationship include the loss of:

- being part of a couple

- having someone to share your day with

- your appetite, sleep, or health

- security—physical or emotional

- control over how the breakup or divorce resolves (having to deal with courts can be especially hard, and, for parents, having to suddenly share custody of children is a huge loss)

People often misunderstand loss, thinking that if it's not the result of a death then the loss isn't hard. That's simply not true. The significance of your loss is based more on personal factors, such as the depth and length of your relationship and how the loss of that relationship impacts other areas of your life. Previous life losses can also surface when a new loss occurs, especially those that weren't fully processed or grieved. This can make things more difficult and leave you feeling like you're buried under a pile of loss.

Healing from Loss

As you focus on grieving your losses—new and old, primary and secondary—you will heal. It may take time, and it will definitely take hard work, but, trust me, you *will* heal.

Bottom Line...

- It is important to identify your losses, both primary and secondary.

- Identifying losses is the first step in grieving them, and that is the beginning of healing.

Tool: Create a Loss Timeline

- ❤ Take a sheet of plain paper and draw a line across the middle. This line represents your life. Ponder the losses in your life, then plot each along the line, according to your age at the time. Include losses like parents' divorce, significant relationships, and also episodes of mental or physical illness; pregnancy loss, financial loss, or moving; and the loss of friends, social status, safety and security, and so on.

- ❤ Examine your loss timeline, adding secondary losses for each primary loss. Try to fully comprehend the loss you have been through so that you're adequately prepared to grieve each one. Discuss your loss timeline with a trusted support person.

11 Grieve.

There is no grief like the grief that does not speak.

—Henry Wadsworth Longfellow

Many of us try to run from grief, but that's like trying to run from a monster sitting on your shoulder. Grief will stay with you until you turn and face it. Once you choose to let yourself go *through* grief, you will feel stronger, healthier, and more confident.

What Is Grief?

Grief is the body's natural response to loss. It can feel physical, with symptoms such as head and body aches, sleep and eating disturbances, and low energy. It can also feel emotional, with symptoms like sadness, crying, cloudy thinking, anxiety, and anger, to name just a few.

Grief, unprocessed, can stick with you for weeks, months, or even years. It can impact your health, your ability to work, your relationships, and definitely your self-esteem. The longer grief has a hold on you, the more likely you are to feel down about yourself, to wonder, "What is wrong with me?" and "Why can't I pull myself together?"

Grief work helps us process what we have been through, make sense of things, and move on after a breakup or loss. It is an expression of love for what has been lost. It is an expression of hope for what might be. Eventually, all loss must be grieved.

The Five Stages of Grief

One of the most well-known models of grief is Elisabeth Kübler-Ross's Five Stages of Grief (Kübler-Ross and Kessler 2005). The five stages of grief are not to be worked through and checked off like a list. Rather, they are guideposts, helping us identify and understand what we feel. Not everyone will experience every stage, and many will go through the stages in a different order. In general, however, grief work will include the following five phases.

Denial

When loss first comes, most of us have a hard time believing that "this is really happening." It's not that we deny the loss, rather, it's a sense that "I just can't believe this person I love isn't going to walk through that door anymore."

This stage includes feelings of shock, numbness, and disbelief, which can also protect us. If we were to take in all the emotion related to the breakup right away, it might be too overwhelming. You may feel the need to tell your story over and over to try and make it seem real. Eventually, you may begin asking questions such as, "How did this happen?" or "Why?" This is a sign you are moving out of denial and through the feeling and healing process.

Anger

Anger can present itself in a variety of ways—anger at your ex, at others, at God, at the world, at yourself. Some will express anger easily and toward anyone or anything; but many of us will instead suppress the anger, keeping it bottled up or even turning it inward toward ourselves.

Anger turned inward is guilt—guilt that we "should have done something" to prevent the breakup, or even guilt about feeling angry toward an ex. But anger is a natural response to loss. Saying, "I'm angry" and letting yourself feel that anger is part of the healing process.

Bargaining

Bargaining comes when we just want life back to the way it used to be. We wish we could go back in time, catch the problems sooner, see something we didn't see. We may also feel guilty, focusing on "If only…"

If the relationship loss was anticipated, bargaining may have been going on for a while—we bargain with God, saying, "I'll do *anything* to keep him here." If the breakup was sudden, we may wish we could go back in time and change things. Bargaining keeps us focused on the past so we don't have to feel the emotions of the present. Bargaining can be helpful, however, as we see what we might have done differently, accept where we are, and move on.

Depression

Eventually, grief will enter on a deeper level, bringing intense feelings of emptiness and sadness. We feel like we don't care about much of anything and wish life would just hurry up and pass on by. Getting out of bed can be a burden, exhaustion and apathy can set in, and we may begin to wonder, "What's the point?"

Others may try to help us out of this "depression," but it's important to understand that bereavement and mourning are not the same as clinical depression. Grief is our body's natural response to loss, not a mental illness. The emotions of the depression stage of grief must be felt and experienced in order for us to heal. (If, however, you begin exhibiting symptoms of clinical depression that intensify or persist after the grief has weakened, please seek help from your medical or mental health provider.)

Acceptance

The experience of depression leads to acceptance. Many people mistakenly believe acceptance means we are "cured" or "all right" with the breakup. This isn't necessarily the case. Though the feelings of loss and grief will eventually lessen, the loss will forever be a part of us, and we will still feel it intermittently. *Acceptance* simply means you are ready to try and move on—to accommodate yourself to this world without your partner.

This process can help you rediscover your sense of self and self-esteem, as you make sense of how life *was* and process how you want life now *to be*.

Bottom Line...

- Grief is common after the loss of a significant relationship.

- The five stages of grief can help you understand your grief, see that it's normal, and navigate the varying symptoms you experience.

Tool: Let Yourself Grieve

♥ Write about your experiences with grief in your journal. Which stage of grief are you currently in? Have you experienced other phases yet? If so, which phases? What was it like going through them?

♥ Talk with a trusted friend or family member about where you are in the grief process. Consult with a grief counselor for additional help.

12 "But how do I grieve?" You just do.

...Grief requires us to turn inward, to go deep into the wilderness of our soul... There is usually no quick way out.

—Dr. Alan D. Wolfelt

I became an expert on grief not just because I've studied it, but because that's what life has given me—many losses. I know how overwhelming, complicated, and scary grief work can be. The most common question I hear about grief and loss is, "How do I grieve?" The answer I give is always the same, "You just do. You *let* yourself grieve."

Grief Work After a Breakup

It's called grief *work* for a reason—it's hard. Many of us fight the emotions of grief, doing whatever it takes to just "be fine." Others distract ourselves from grief by keeping busy or escaping into activities. Some of us simply ignore the emotions of grief, pretending everything is okay.

Grief work, or mourning, is the process of letting oneself go *through* the emotions of grief. *Through* is the only way *out*. One model I find particularly helpful in grief work is Worden's Four Tasks of

Mourning (2008). This model looks at grief work not as emotions or stages to be experienced but rather as tasks to be worked through.

Let's explore each of these tasks a little further.

1. Accept the reality of the loss.

For most, it will take time to accept the reality of a significant breakup or divorce. To help with this task, let yourself think about and process your breakup and related losses as often as you need. Tell your story in a safe environment. Let yourself *FEEL* the emotions of grief. This will help you begin to accept what you have lost.

2. Experience the pain of grief.

This is the task with which many of us have the hardest time, and the one to which most are referring when they ask, "*How* do I grieve?" We fear that if we start feeling the mix of emotions inside, we may never untangle ourselves from them. Experiencing the pain of grief is the only way to complete the other tasks and to heal. As we allow the emotions of grief to arise and express themselves in healthy ways, little by little, we become free of the intense pain of loss. As I said before, *through* is the only way *out*.

To facilitate feeling the emotions of grief, I have created a model I call TEARS. This model provides five ideas for how to grieve, each of which is equally helpful in the healing process.

TEARS

- **Talking:** Talking gets the story and emotions out of you. It also helps by sharing the burden of grief with your family, friends, or other support people.

- **Exercise:** Physical activity helps release the difficult emotions that accompany loss. Exercise "allows for a reduction of aggressive feelings, a release of tension and anxiety, and a relief of depression" related to grief (Rando 1984, 57).

- **Artistic expression:** For many, grief is best expressed creatively—through art, music, dance, and more. Tapping your creative outlets allows you to process the emotions of grief in a subconscious way that can be powerful.

- **Recording emotions and experiences:** Write about your experiences with grief. Getting the feelings out of you and onto paper is an excellent way to process and allows you to leave your grief and return to it later as needed. Journaling ensures we do not miss the important lessons being taught.

- **Sobbing:** There is healing power in allowing our tears to flow. As Washington Irving once said, "There is sacredness in tears. They are not the mark of weakness—but of power."

3. Adjust to the environment from which your ex is missing.

The TEARS method can also help you through tasks 3 and 4, as you adjust to the environment from which your ex is missing and reinvest in new relationships. Adjustment takes time and will come as you continually work through the emotions of grief. It involves *allowing* yourself to adjust, learning to *let go*, and being *willing* to move on when you feel ready.

4. Withdraw emotional energy and reinvest it in another relationship.

Eventually, you *will* feel ready to reinvest in other relationships. This might mean becoming closer to your family members, bonding in new ways with old friends or making new friends, or discovering healthy, new, intimate relationships.

Dealing with Grief Takes Time

Some factors can make grief last longer—like failing to acknowledge your losses, ignoring grief work, or continuing unhealthy contact with your ex. My advice is to dig in and do your grief work now. Remind yourself: "As long as I am working on my grief, the grief work is working." Give yourself time, space, and all the love you can muster to nurture yourself through the work of grief.

Bottom Line...

- Worden's Four Tasks of Mourning can guide you through your grief work.

- The TEARS method can show you *how* to grieve.

Tool: Begin Your Grief Work

♥ Set aside thirty minutes to an hour to actively grieve today, using one (or more) of the TEARS methods discussed earlier. Use a timer, if needed, and give yourself permission to put the grief away when the time is up.

♥ Acknowledge any confounding factors that may make grieving more difficult (for example, continued unhealthy contact with your ex, not feeling you have space to grieve because of your kids or responsibilities). Using your support system or a counselor, work on a plan to resolve these issues.

13 Tackle your broken thoughts.

Our life is what our thoughts make it.

—Marcus Aurelius

One of the best things I've ever discovered is the relationship between my thoughts, feelings, body, and behavior—and how to change my thinking. This chapter presents Aaron Beck's cognitive behavioral therapy (1976) in a nutshell. I hope it becomes one of the best things you've ever learned, too.

The Power of Thought Management

It's estimated that we humans have an average of 60,000 thoughts per day. Were you aware you were thinking so much? Probably not. A vast majority of these thoughts are what we call "automatic thoughts"—they come without any conscious effort on our part. And, just like a fish doesn't know it's in water, we can be so immersed in automatic thoughts that we don't even hear them. Unfortunately, many of our automatic thoughts are "broken," meaning they are neither healthy nor helpful. Often, the thoughts we think aren't even true.

The problem is that our thoughts are linked to our body, emotions, and behaviors. Even untrue thoughts can set off a cycle of emotions and behavioral reactions, leaving us feeling out of control. Learning to see the connections between thoughts, feelings, bodily responses, and behaviors empowers us.

Understanding the Thought Cycle

Allow me to explain how this works. Life presents us with situations. For example, your boyfriend of four years suddenly texts you "It's over," then refuses to answer your calls. Automatic thoughts arise: "No! I can't handle this! I need you! Don't leave!" These thoughts create a physiological response: your blood pressure rises, your pulse increases, your heart rate speeds up, and adrenaline pumps through your body. Almost simultaneously, an emotion appears, or several emotions. You feel pain, panic, and fear. You then engage in a behavior. In this case, you pull yourself together enough to call your best girlfriend, she comes over, and you talk and cry with her all night long.

In the morning, you realize he wasn't very good to you anyway. After all, what kind of guy dumps you in a text message without another word? You've been raised to believe in yourself and to trust your instincts, and now you see clearly that you really will be better off without him. What are your next thoughts? Perhaps, "I can do this! It's going to be tough, but I know this is right." Your parasympathetic nervous system kicks in—your heart rate slows, pulse lowers, and breathing settles into a more natural pattern. You feel some sadness and worry, but also relief and comfort, knowing you're doing the right thing. And your behavior? You celebrate by going out for an ice-cream cone with your girlfriend, to reward your courage and honesty.

But let's say you've been raised to believe you are "unlovable." In this case, the morning after you vent to your girlfriend, your thoughts might sound like, "It's all my fault. I've messed things up again. This proves it—I really am impossible to love. He may not have been good for me, but he was better than nothing!" Your body responds by keeping the cortisol and adrenaline flowing, your stomach becomes upset from the tension, and your breathing remains fast and shallow. Your emotions include anxiety, fear, grief, and self-loathing. And your behavior? You go and eat an entire *carton* of ice cream as a form of self-punishment.

It's All Connected

Learning about cognitive behavioral theory, we see that not only are thoughts, feelings, the body, and behavior connected, they are influenced by the thoughts, feelings, and behaviors of our past. Our present thoughts also influence our *future* behavior. Once we understand this, we can break into this cycle of thoughts, feelings, body, and behavior—and make a change.

Bottom Line...

- Your thoughts, feelings, body, and behavior are connected.

- Understanding this thought cycle gives us a chance to intervene and make a change.

Tool: Notice the Thought Cycle in Your Everyday Life

❤ Look for connections between your thoughts, feelings, body, and behavior in your everyday experiences. Observe how your thoughts influence your present and future behavior. Ponder how your past plays a role in your present feelings, thoughts, and behavior. Write it all down in your journal or notebook.

14 What are you thinking?

It's not who you are that holds you back,
it's who you think you're not.

—Hanoch McCarty (attributed)

Can you see the power that listening to and altering your thoughts might have on your life? Imagine being free of racing thoughts about your ex. Or being free of the emotions associated with worrying about your future. Imagine preventing future pain or suffering simply because you have conquered your thoughts.

Through practice, we can train ourselves to pay attention to important thoughts—to glean valuable nuggets of truth about how we feel, what we need, and, ultimately, who we are. Then, we can choose to let the rest go. Changing our thoughts can have a profound effect on our feelings, body, and behavioral responses as well, freeing us from pain, sorrow, and so much more.

Change Your Thoughts, Change Your Life

Of course, it's hard to do at first. Like any new skill, it takes practice to hear, challenge, and change unhealthy thoughts, so it's best to start small.

- **Start by trying to *hear* what you've been telling yourself lately about your breakup and your self-esteem.** Stop and listen when you feel the heartache, pain, anger, or grief. What are you saying to yourself? How is it related to your emotions? How does it affect your body? Do your thoughts help or hurt you in the long run? Are they truthful or exaggerated? Are you hard on yourself, tearing yourself down? Or are your thoughts loving, nurturing you body, mind, and soul?

- **Notice the impact that your thoughts are having on your life.** Do you ever catch yourself engaging in unhealthy behavior because of an automatic thought? For instance, driving by your ex's apartment just to see if he's there, even though you know it always hurts to see his new girlfriend's car in the parking lot? (Yes, I know that one from past experience!) Do your thoughts lead you toward healthy feelings and activities, or do they keep you stuck?

- **Pay attention to how your past influences your present thoughts.** Do you hear worries that stem from before your breakup (e.g., "He hates it when I go out with friends, so I'd better not")? Are your past fears controlling your present behavior (e.g., "I was afraid I'd lose him, and I did, so I won't ever put myself out there again")? Can you see how your future might continue to be influenced by your broken thinking if you don't take the time to make a few repairs? Can you see how, if you do learn to hear and alter your thinking, it has the potential to significantly change your life?

Are you ready to give it a try?

Bottom Line...

- Once you hear your thoughts and begin to see how they influence your life, then you can choose to change your thoughts.

- In changing your thoughts, you have the potential to significantly change your life.

Tool: Learn to Hear Your Thoughts

♥ Use the questions above to explore the connection among your thoughts, feelings, body, and behavior. When you feel a powerful emotion, stop and pay attention to what you are thinking. Write it down.

♥ Ask yourself, "In what ways do my thoughts create my sense of self and self-esteem?" "How are my thoughts contributing to my distress over my breakup?" "How might changing my thoughts change my life?"

15 Stop the broken record.

Drag your thoughts away from your troubles...by the ears, by the heels, or any other way you can manage it.

—Mark Twain

Unheard automatic thoughts tend to play in our minds like a broken record. They repeat the same old messages: "I'm not good enough." "I can't handle this." "Everyone leaves me."

The good news is that we can work on our thoughts. We can learn to hear them, as we discussed in chapter 14. We also have the power to manage and change our thoughts. One of the best approaches I've discovered for thought management is a little tool I love called the "thought record."

Thought Management

Your thoughts are all over the place. They're racing and whirling and overwhelming you. Yet you need to listen to what they're saying. And to do this, you need to organize your thoughts. One of the best ways to manage your thoughts is with a thought record.

Initially, a thought record helps us notice automatic thoughts, prompts us to write them down, and compels us to tease them apart from emotions. In time, a thought record can also help us identify false beliefs and change them into something more truthful and helpful. In this chapter, let's focus on the first steps of using a thought record: learning to identify difficult situations, thoughts, and emotions.

Use a thought record when worry, anger, fear, or any other powerful emotion overcomes you. It can also be used for positive emotions too, such as happiness, peace, or inspiration. The purpose of the thought record is to help you better understand your situations, thoughts, and feelings—and how they're all related. It also gets the thoughts and emotions out of your head and onto paper, stopping the broken record that keeps playing in your mind and causing you distress. Let's get started!

Thought Record, Part 1

Pull out your journal or a sheet of paper (or open a blank text file). Orient the paper or text file horizontally and create a table with five columns. Label the top of each column: Date, Situation, Automatic Thoughts, Emotions, and Rating. Alternatively, you can download and print a PDF of Thought Record Part 1 at http://www.whoami withoutyou.com with the columns already labeled. And for a little more assistance, visit http://www.whoamiwithoutyou.com to see a video of how to fill out a Thought Record. Now follow these steps:

1. *Date.* In the first column, write the date.

2. *Situation.* In the second column, write a brief description of what's going on. For example, "I was at work and got a text from my ex." Just write enough so that you remember what was happening at the time your emotions started taking over.

3. *Automatic Thoughts.* Now, stop. Before writing down your thoughts in the third column, listen to what's going on in your head. What are you thinking about this situation? Write out each sentence as you hear it; list as many as you can. For example, you might start off hearing, "Why is he texting me? He's not supposed to bother me at work." If you listen more closely, you hear, "I'm getting really fed up with him breaking the rules!" Then, "I can't handle this!" Try to hear and write down everything.

4. *Emotions.* In the fourth column, list your emotions—there are usually more than one. You might know you feel frustrated and angry, but is there a hint of sadness in there, too? What about exhaustion? Identifying as many emotions as you're feeling helps you begin to tease them apart.

5. *Rating.* In the final column, rate your emotions from 1 to 10, with 10 being the most extreme and 1 being no big deal.

That's it. In the next chapter you'll learn how to challenge some of the thoughts, but for now it's good enough that you got them out of your head and onto paper.

Tips for Using the Thought Record, Part 1

Keep in mind:

- **It's hard to hear automatic thoughts at first.** If you're not used to it, be patient. It often helps to talk out your situations and have someone else help you identify your thoughts. Cognitive behavioral therapy (CBT) is great for this—clients bring empty thought records to me and we fill them out together. It's easy for me to hear and write their thoughts as they tell the story. I highly recommend it if you need help.

- **Most people have a hard time distinguishing thoughts from feelings.** Thoughts and feelings can feel like a jumbled mess in your head, and it can be tough to tease them apart. It's much easier to deal with thoughts and emotions when you can see them as the separate entities they are. The thought record helps you work on this.

- **As you work on it, you'll begin to notice patterns of thoughts and feelings.** Certain feelings will keep coming up and will usually be related to the same types of thoughts. You will realize how often you're dealing with the same old things, which can be very motivating.

- **Over time, you'll be able to pull out "themes" from your thoughts.** For instance, you might always automatically go to the belief that you're "not good enough," or that "everyone always abandons" you, or that "life is against" you. It's good to know what these themes are, for then you'll have the opportunity to challenge and change them.

- **Eventually, you'll be able to hear the automatic thoughts and beliefs, challenge them, and change them while you're still in the situation, or even before the situation gets started.** Yep, eventually, if you work on it, you *will*. How's that for changing your life?

Bottom Line…

- A thought record is the perfect tool to help you stop, hear, and begin to challenge your thoughts.

- It takes time to master your thinking, but believe me: it is worth the effort. I still use these skills every day, and, with practice, you will too.

Tool: Learn to Use the Thought Record, Part 1

♥   For one week, practice using the Thought Record, Part 1. Refer to the instructions given in this chapter as you need to. Next, we're going to alter those thoughts, but, for now, get comfortable hearing them, separating them from feelings, and writing them down.

16 Change your mind.

The mind is everything.
What you think, you become.

—Buddha (attributed)

Ready to change your mind? I don't mean changing your mind about the breakup. I mean changing your *thoughts*. Your mind is made up of thoughts, after all. Now that you've learned how to *hear* your thoughts (chapters 13 and 14) and tease them apart from your emotions (chapter 15), it's time to challenge and change them.

Challenge Your Thoughts

Hopefully you've been practicing part 1 of the thought record for at least a few days, and, ideally, for a week or longer. The more you've practiced, the better. If you feel like you're getting the hang of pulling out your thought record when things get intense and sorting through your thoughts and feelings on paper, then you're ready for part 2.

Part 2 asks you to do additional work by going deeper into examining your thoughts, so that you can find the truth in them. The point of part 2 is to help you challenge irrational thinking, find a thought that's more helpful, and make change.

Thought Record, Part 2

Part 2 of the Thought Record builds on part 1 by adding two more columns. These extra steps take you further into managing your thoughts and understanding which are helpful and unhelpful. To begin, pull out your completed Thought Record Part 1 and add two more columns, or grab a fresh sheet of paper and create seven columns. You can also download and print a PDF of part 2 from http://www.whoami withoutyou.com, and watch a video explanation of how to use it. (For a little more help, a video that guides you in filling out part 2 of the Thought Record is available on the same site.)

1. *Fill out the first five columns.* Refer to the Thought Record, Part 1 exercise in chapter 15 for instructions.

2. *Challenge each automatic thought.* Go through each thought listed in the Automatic Thoughts column and ask yourself, "Is this truthful?" or better yet, "Is this helpful?" This is where we discover what I like to call "the truth." You're not trying to simply flip a negative into a positive here. You're trying to be *honest.* Some thoughts may be truthful and helpful already. For example, if you wrote, "I don't like dealing with my ex," that is the truth. Underline all of the thoughts that are already true. Other thoughts, however, will be irrational, such as "I'm going to die if I have to hear about him going out with that woman one more time!" Are you really going to die? No. So, what *is* the truth? Circle those thoughts that are not truthful; we will use these in the next step.

3. *Rational or Alternative Response.* Once you've identified which thoughts are untrue, you can work on a more rational, truthful, or alternative response in this new column. Using our previous example, you might write, "I'm not going to die, but it hurts so much to hear about him with that other woman. It makes me want to cry." That's the truth, and it can lead to actually crying and then talking about the situation rather than getting dramatic.

4. *Outcome.* Now, in the second new column, revisit each emotion you listed and re-rate how strong it is, with 1 being weak and 10 being powerful. After finding the rational or alternative response, you'll usually find that your emotions become less intense.

Changing Your Mind Takes Time

When trying to change your mind using Thought Records Parts 1 and 2, remember:

- **It takes time to learn these skills.** Don't think that just because you're working on it, you're going to change every harmful thought immediately. Give yourself time to keep practicing.

- **The point is to discover those thoughts that help you feel better but are also based on the truth.** Again, you're not just looking for affirmations or flipping a negative into a positive. You're trying to understand whether your thoughts are helping you or not. And if they're not, you're looking for the truth—for alternative ways to see, feel, and think. You don't have to believe "the truth" yet; just see it.

- **It can be useful to have a friend, loved one, or support person help you find the rational response.** She or he can offer new ways to look at things and inspire a new way to think.

- **It's hard to believe something false once you've proven to yourself it's not true.** If you always say, "I can't handle this," for instance, it's hard to buy in to it after you've proven, "Really, I can. I'm just tired of dealing with it, and I need a break."

Bottom Line…

- If your automatic thoughts are neither helpful nor truthful, you can search for the truth and replace it with an alternative thought.

- Changing your thoughts by finding the alternative or rational response can also change your feelings, decreasing their intensity and leading to healthier behavior.

Tool: Practice Using the Thought Record, Part 2

- ♥ For at least one week, practice with the Thought Record, Part 2, following the directions above. Work on the alternative responses and try to replace your unhealthy thoughts as often as possible.

- ♥ Check in with yourself after the week is over to review your responses and look for common themes. This will get you ready for the next chapter.

17 Get a new view and a new you.

If you don't change your beliefs, your life will be like this forever. Is that good news?

—William Somerset Maugham

Once we hear, write down, and alter our thoughts, like we learned to do in chapters 14 through 16, we can look for patterns. We begin to see the overarching themes that influence how we view the world. We see how our beliefs affect how we feel and shape who we think we are. We see that our beliefs are at the core of our worldview.

But are we always right in what we believe—about the world, about others, about ourselves? Could it be that some of our beliefs need an overhaul just as much as some of our thoughts do? Could it be that a new view awaits, and could that mean a new *you* awaits, too?

Understanding Beliefs

The field of psychology calls our pattern of thoughts and beliefs our "schema." The term has been around for centuries, originally discussed by philosopher Immanuel Kant and then introduced into science and psychology by Jean Piaget. A person's schema refers to his or her underlying beliefs about him- or herself, others, and the world. Some of our schemas develop as a result of our upbringing; we may adopt many of our parents' beliefs and views. Others arise from life experiences.

Either way, one's schema may be helpful or unhelpful. If I were raised to believe in my true worth, to feel loved unconditionally, to feel valued and important, then that schema would be helpful—one I would want to keep. If, on the other hand, I were raised to believe I'm worthless, unimportant, and insignificant, then it's probable that schema has caused me years of heartache and pain. I would therefore want to work on changing it.

Schemas, or beliefs, are typically harder to change than individual thoughts. But they *are* changeable. I know this is true—not just because the research says so, but because I've worked with many people over the years who have made significant changes to their thoughts and feelings *as well as* their beliefs.

Not only *can* you change your beliefs, it's a useful skill to develop if you want a life of love and joy. Much of the time it's our outdated and often harmful beliefs that are keeping us stuck. Nowhere is this truer than when someone struggles with self-worth. We believe we are unlovable. We believe we are inadequate. Yet these beliefs are simply not true. They're merely ancient schemas we've picked up along the way—and it's time to let them go.

How to Change Your Beliefs

Now that you're a pro at using a thought record, we're going to implement it in changing your beliefs.

1. **Revisit your thought records and look for common themes.** When I help clients with this, my evaluation of their thought records might go something like, "In this situation you're telling yourself, 'I can't handle my life.' In this situation, you say, 'I'm a loser,' and in this one, you say, 'I'm not

good enough for him.' There's a definite theme of feeling inadequate, wouldn't you agree?" Identify commonalities in what you've written on your thought records.

2. **Write down the "theme" or "schema" in your own words.** In the example above, I would ask the client to help me come up with the right words for her schema. It might be a theme of inadequacy, or feeling incapable, or it might be something like, "The world is against me." It's helpful for you to label your schema in your *own* words, making sure it feels true to you.

3. **Challenge your schema.** Ask yourself, "What proof do I have of this belief?" For instance, if your schema is "I'm unlovable," then ask yourself, "What proof do I have that I'm unlovable?" You might come up with examples such as, "Well, my dad left us when I was young, and then my first boyfriend cheated on me. Now my husband has abandoned me. It must be because I'm unlovable." Drag out all your evidence and write it down.

4. **Investigate the authenticity of your "proof" by looking for alternatives.** You have all this "evidence," but is it as solid as you believe? Search out alternative ways to see things. Imagine you're someone else—your neighbor, your pastor, your support person. How might he or she view things? Be willing to see all possibilities, even if you don't believe them right now. Going back to our example above, you might discover, "I suppose it's *possible* all these men left me because I'm unlovable, but it's also possible they left because *they* don't know how to love."

5. **Change the schema to "the truth" or an alternative.** We'll work more on how to let yourself believe something new as we discuss discovering self-worth in the chapters to come. For now, try to change one little belief that's been holding you back. Write it down so you don't forget it.

Bottom Line...

- Faulty beliefs, called schemas, are at the core of our most challenging life struggles.

- Identifying and challenging schemas can open you up to a new view of others, the world around you, and, yes, *yourself.*

Tool: Identify and Challenge Each Schema

- ♥ Create a list of your core values and beliefs. Do the thoughts you're discovering on your thought records match up with those beliefs and values? Are the schemas you're discovering in line with who and how you would like to be?

- ♥ Using your thought records, search for themes of overarching beliefs. Apply the steps above to challenge each schema you discover. Investigate for new proof, and work on changing each unhealthy belief.

18 Face your fears.

There is no illusion greater than fear.

—Lao-tzu

After a breakup or divorce, it's common to feel afraid. You may fear having to deal with your ex. You may fear how your breakup will impact your family, friends, or children. You may fear that you'll never find love again.

Just because fear is a common emotion after a breakup, however, doesn't mean you have to live with it. Learning how to overcome fear is one of the most important life lessons. So, take a deep breath, and let's put that fear back in its place—out of your heart and back under the dark rock from whence it came.

Fear Doesn't Prevent Bad, It Prevents Good

Fear prevents good; that's what I've learned. It's an inhibitor. It stops us in our tracks. It keeps us from doing the things that actually might benefit us.

Most people have it backward; they think, "Fear prevents *bad* things from happening." They think fear is a signal, telling them something terrible is going to happen if they don't stop in their tracks right now! It's true that, historically, our ancestors relied upon fear to warn them of dangers that were real and present. Fortunately, most of us no longer live in such a physically threatening world. Unfortunately, many of us still experience and react to fear, even though most of the time the danger is neither real nor present.

Often, the danger is in our minds: fears of more loss, loneliness, pain, and heartache; fears of flying, speaking, losing, and failing; fear of not being enough; even fear of success and all the change that goes with it. The list goes on! When we heed the voices of fear, we stop. We panic. We lose our focus. And we ultimately prevent ourselves from engaging in the very goals we so desire to achieve.

Remove Fear's Power

How does fear show up in *your* life? If you can recognize fear for what it is, you can choose to stop letting fear have its way with you.

I, like you, know fear firsthand. I've felt that familiar catch in my chest more times than I care to admit. I feel fear when my kids make poor choices, or when I think of one of my family members dying. I feel fear when starting a new endeavor, or when faced with a life challenge I'm not sure I can handle. As I've worked on fear, however, I've learned to hear and distinguish its voice from mine. Fear is the one trying to stop me from doing those things that scare me *but* are *good* for me. When I hear the voice of fear, I can choose to expose it. I can choose to feel the emotion of fear and do the thing that scares me anyway—or not—based on my own conscience and not on the overwhelming *feeling* of fear. Exposing fear—naming and feeling it—is what takes its power away.

Fear vs. Warning

You may be thinking, "But people *do* die, and fail, and horrible things happen," and you'd be right. But giving in to fear doesn't help. Feeling afraid doesn't *prevent* the bad things from happening.

There's a difference between *fear* and a *warning*. When we are spiritually in tune, we may experience warnings that prevent us from harm. You've likely experienced this yourself, but if you haven't, you've no doubt heard others tell stories of receiving a warning that prevented them from driving a certain way or getting on a plane or allowing their kids to do a certain activity. Later, they recognized that they had prevented a great tragedy or harm. These are remarkable experiences, but the thing to focus on here is how people describe these experiences. They say, "I just felt like I shouldn't go" or "I had this overwhelming feeling I needed to turn around." This has been my experience as well—an overwhelming feeling telling me what I must do, a feeling I listen to because it feels *right*.

Now, think of fear. Every one of us has experienced moments of fear. Some moments may have existed mostly in our minds, such as the fear of performing. Some may have been physically threatening, like almost falling, getting injured, or coming close to death. Either way, the experience was likely the same: blood pressure went up, the heart started to race, sensation may have been lost in the extremities, including dizziness or lightheadedness. It likely felt out of your control; you were probably literally *unable* to control certain aspects of your body. It did not feel good. It did not feel "right." You did not, most likely, even *want* to be feeling what you felt. You wanted it to be *over*. Quite a different experience than those moments of warning, right?

How to Not Let Fear Get the Better of You

The next time you feel afraid, stop and ask yourself, "Is this a true warning? Or is this just the emotion of fear?" Name it for what it is. Fear can't keep you afraid if you expose it. It can't prevent you from doing something that feels scary but is good for you if you stop, name it, and feel it.

Increase your attention to warnings. Listen and heed them. But *decrease* your attention to fear. The only two things fear is good for are noticing the attempt it will make to prevent you from moving forward, and recognizing that you're probably onto something really good. Then, you can thank the fear for that understanding and wish it well as you walk on by.

Bottom Line...

- Fear doesn't prevent *bad*, it prevents *good*.

- Learning to differentiate between fear and a warning can help you take the power away from your fears.

Tool: Eliminate Your Fears

- ♥ Expose your fears. List them all in your journal. Use a thought record to seek out any lingering fears that may be holding you back.

- ♥ Feel the fear. It sounds scary, but sitting and feeling the fear helps you realize it's just an emotion. It takes the power back. Use the tools from chapter 7 to help you as needed.

- ♥ Let the fear go. After you've seen it for what it is, you have a choice. Will you cling to your fears? Or will you see how they are holding you back and choose to let them go?

19 You are more than your relationships.

We cannot think of being acceptable to others until we have first proven acceptable to ourselves.

—Malcolm X

We often place our value in relationships, especially intimate ones. Being "the girlfriend of so-and-so" or "the wife of so-and-so" becomes part of our identity. When intimate relationships end, our sense of who we are—our self-worth, how we feel about ourselves, our self-esteem—takes a hit. We may feel abandoned, not good enough, or, at the very least, our identity may be shaken, making us wonder, "What does this breakup mean about *me*? Am I good enough for anyone?"

The need for connection and belonging is also a significant part of who we are and, thus, a significant factor in our self-esteem. Research has shown that we are hardwired for connection— emotionally, psychologically, physically, and spiritually (B. Brown 2012). When those connections or our relationships are severed, it cuts to our core, making us question our identity, who we are, and whether we will ever be good enough.

The Truth About Your Breakup, Identity, and Self-Worth

We are more than our relationships. That's the truth. We are innately lovable, worthy, important, valuable, and good. Yes, I mean *you*. You are all these things, and you are definitely good enough. If you're not convinced, we'll discuss this in greater detail in part 2, but, for now, just trust me—you are more than what others think, say, or do to you. We all are.

We mustn't let what others say about us or do to us become who we are. We can certainly learn from mistakes we've made in our relationships, but we mustn't let those mistakes become our identity. It's hard, though, isn't it? It's hard to weed through all that your ex has said and done to you, to discover what is true and what is not. It's hard to know what to believe when your sense of self-worth is caught up in the loss of your relationship.

Teasing Out the Truth

How can you begin to figure out the truth—to tease apart your identity from what has happened to you? Let's begin with the following:

- **List all the thoughts you've heard from others about the breakup.** Write down what you think it means about your identity. Don't hold back. Be honest. Get it out so that you can get to work. Oh, and be sure to list the positives as well.

- **Use a thought record to challenge the thoughts you've heard and search for alternative interpretations.** List these alternatives in the "rational or alternative response" column. Remember, there are always other ways of seeing things. Ask your parents, siblings, friends, and coworkers to tell you how they view your breakup, if you need help. Then listen and let their words inspire you to come up with your own alternative responses. Ask yourself, "What does this *really* mean about who I am?"

- **Look for the lessons in your breakup and be willing to learn from them.** If you hear things you don't like about yourself, be willing to explore and work on them. For instance, maybe you realize you were "a doormat" with your ex. You don't like it and want to change. That's good. Instead of turning that thought into a negative schema that wrecks your self-image (e.g., "I can't stand up for myself. I'm a wimp"), see it as a weakness to be strengthened. (We'll work more on strengthening weaknesses in chapter 27.)

- **Let the rest go.** If you've looked at everything and learned what needs to be learned, let the rest go. Trust me—it's not worth holding on to the lies you or your ex have told you about who you are. Let them go.

Dare to believe you are good enough. Then be willing to get out there and prove it to yourself.

Bottom Line...

- Our relationships are usually intertwined with our identity, which can significantly impact our sense of self-worth and leave us wondering, "Am I good enough?"

- We are more than our relationships, and tackling unhealthy beliefs is the way to see the truth—to discover strengths, improve weaknesses, and let the rest go.

Tool: What Does This Breakup Mean About You?

♥ Use the steps in this chapter to tackle thoughts, feelings, and beliefs about your identity after your breakup. Ask yourself, "What does this breakup mean about me?" Write down your initial impressions as you would your automatic thoughts on a thought record.

♥ Next, find the alternative or rational response. Ask yourself, "What does this breakup *really* mean about me, my identity, and who I truly am?" Write down all possibilities. See if your beliefs have changed.

20 Get your self-esteem back.

A successful [person] is one who can
lay a firm foundation with the bricks
that others throw at him [or her].

—David Brinkley

After a breakup, it can feel like your ex stole your self-esteem. Trust me, he didn't. The feeling is only temporary, because no one can take what is only yours to give. He might be able to plant doubts in your mind, or cloud up your emotions, or treat you in ways that make you wonder if you'll ever find love again (or if it's even worth it), but he can't steal your self-esteem or sense of self-worth.

It's All Up to You

This is great news, because if only *you* can give away your self-esteem, then only *you* can bring it back. Only *you* decide which thoughts and feelings you allow about yourself. Only *you* label those thoughts and feelings. Only *you* have the key to open up your heart or lock it away for good. Only *you*.

Only you can decide if you want more—if you want better. You can decide you want a relationship that inspires the best in you, that is unconditional, that is pure. You can discover that you want this relationship not just with someone else but also with yourself.

Yes, it's all up to you. You can choose to stay where you are, feeling broken by your breakup, or you can choose to move forward, rediscovering your true worth and rebuilding your self-esteem. I know, it sounds easier than it really is—believing the good stuff about yourself and letting go of all the—well, for lack of a better word—*crud*. But it *is* possible.

Again, here's the great news: *you* get to decide how you feel about yourself—not your ex, your friends, your family, or anyone else. Only you. You can start now by believing what I'm saying, by believing in your strength. You can become the person you've always known you are. You can love yourself, realize your true potential, and fulfill your life's purpose.

That's what part 2 of this book is all about, so stick with me. It's going to be a fabulous ride.

Bottom Line...

- It can feel like your self-esteem is gone when a valued relationship ends.

- Only you can decide to bring that self-esteem back, and part 2 of this book will show you how.

Tool: Get Honest About Your Self-Esteem

- ♥ Ask yourself, "In what way has my breakup impacted my self-esteem?" "How do I feel about myself now, compared to before my breakup?" "Do I feel like my self-esteem was lost or stolen?" "Do I believe I can get it back?"

- ♥ Write down your answers. Be as honest as you can. Then get ready to get to work in part 2.

Part 2

Building Unwavering Self-Esteem

Moving On and Uncovering the Real You

21 Lay a mindful foundation.

Ultimately, mindfulness can become an effortless,
seamless element of our life, a way for our very being
to express itself authentically, with integrity.

—Jon Kabat-Zinn

In part 1, we focused on skills of *over*coming—overcoming the grief, worry, anger, and fear of your breakup; overcoming negative thoughts and beliefs. Now we shift to *be*coming—becoming your true self, living authentically, becoming in tune with your divine purpose and potential, and, ultimately, building unwavering self-esteem. Though both are important and helpful, *be*coming involves a whole different energy than *over*coming. It involves getting still, listening, and paying attention at a deeper level. It involves mindful living.

The Benefits of Mindfulness

Mindfulness is "paying attention…on purpose, in the present moment, and non-judgmentally," Jon Kabat-Zinn writes (2012, 17). It involves using our senses to focus on the world before, in, and all around us. Research shows that those who practice mindfulness have less stress, better health, and overall more positive moods (Brown and Ryan 2003). Mindfulness helps us to focus on what matters most and to let go of the unnecessary things, simplifying life and bringing greater peace.

Mindfulness may involve breathing, pondering, meditation, and stillness. It can get you away from your breakup and all your mind has to say about it, and into your spirit and soul, where the true wisdom lies. Before we can work on unwavering self-esteem, it's important to lay a proper foundation using the skills of mindfulness.

How to Begin a Mindfulness Practice

Like I said, mindfulness may include a variety of different practices, and it is up to you to decide which ones are most beneficial. I encourage you to at least *try* each of the following practices. You might be surprised at how beneficial they can be for you.

Breathing

Deep breathing is an important element of not just mindfulness—it's part of cognitive behavioral treatment, stress-reduction programs, and, yes, spiritual practices as well. Breathing on purpose is one of the simplest yet most effective skills you can learn to reduce tension and stress, increase peace and energy, and slow yourself down for better relaxation and sleep. You can watch a demonstration of this exercise online at http://www.whoamiwithoutyou.com.

Sit comfortably in a chair or lie down. Relax your body, but keep your mind alert. Place one hand on your belly and one on your chest. Breathe normally. You may notice that, as you inhale, your chest rises and your belly falls. This is how most of us breathe most of the time—from the chest. Now, as you inhale, try to fill your belly with as much air as possible. As you exhale, feel it force its way out and up through your chest. If you're doing this right, the hand on your belly should rise on the inhale while the hand on your chest falls or stays the same. Slowly inhale for ten counts. Then exhale for ten. Repeat ten times.

Be sure to use your newfound breathing skills when powerful emotions come your way. Breathing is an excellent way to cope with and FEEL emotions.

Focus on the Now

One of my favorite ways to focus on the now is to go for a walk. You can walk around your house or workplace if you can't get outdoors, but if you can get out, I highly recommend it.

As you walk, use each of your five senses to take in the world around you. What do you see? What do you hear? Smell? Taste? Feel? Take it all in and just let it be, without judgment or conversation. Simply be where you are.

Apply this technique when you get caught up in overthinking. Stop, and use all your senses to take in the present moment. Usually, you'll find that whatever issue your mind was grappling with isn't as catastrophic as it may have seemed.

Meditation

There are many ways to meditate, and no one right way to do it. To begin, let's learn a simple mindful meditation.

Sit in a comfortable position. You may want to sit on the floor with your legs crossed or in a cozy chair. Take three deep breaths, as instructed in the Breathing exercise. As you breathe normally, focus your attention on your thoughts. Watch the thoughts float through your mind as you would birds flying in the sky. Let each thought pass by and do not judge. If you get stuck on a thought, simply notice it and let it go. The point isn't to "try not to think." It's to *notice* the thoughts as they come and go, to get used to hearing and seeing them, while not getting stuck on them. No matter what passes through your mind, you can choose to let it go. Do this for five minutes the first day, working up to ten, then fifteen or more each day.

Bottom Line...

- Mindfulness pulls us out of the past and future and helps us focus on the present moment.

- Practicing mindfulness through deep breathing, focusing on the present, and meditating can open the door to less stress, greater energy, better moods, and more peace. It can also open the door to who we really are.

Tool: Practice Mindfulness

- ♥ Select one or more of the mindfulness practices in this chapter and try it today. Write about the experience in your journal. Remember: these skills, like all skills, take practice to master. Commit to practicing mindfulness every day for the next week. See how you feel after the week is done, and write about it.

22 Ask yourself, "Who am I?"

What a liberation to realize that the "voice in my head" is not who I am. Who am I then? The one who sees that.

—Eckhart Tolle

I've asked clients and friends (and myself) many times, and I've heard all kinds of answers—"I'm a single mom," "I'm an optimist," "I'm a doctor," "I'm an eternal soul," "I'm trying to figure that out." It's how we introduce ourselves to people: "My name is _____ and I work as a _____ and I like doing _____." For many, it's easy to answer: "I'm a short, blonde artist." "I'm a mom, a nurse, and I have a passion for scrapbooking." For others, it's not so easy: "It's something I ask myself all the time." "I'm not sure who I am yet, but I am learning."

The way I see it, there are two ways to answer the question "Who am I?": 1) with our head and heart, or 2) with our soul. The head and heart tell us some facts about who we are, but it's the soul that answers the question, "Yes, but who are you, *really?*"

Who You Are Not

Let's look at who you are by shedding some light on who you're *not*.

You Are Not How You Look

Short or tall, fair or dark, thin or not-so-thin—these describe your body. But are *you* your body? No. It's part of you, but it's definitely only part of the story.

You Are Not How You Feel

How about your feelings? They can certainly be powerful; at times, it can seem like *they* are *you*. Yet, emotions arise from all kinds of things—the weather, hormones, sleep or lack thereof, challenges, blessings. We've already discussed how emotions may come or go like the weather (chapter 7). You are so much more than your emotions.

You Are Not What You Think

What about your thoughts? Our thoughts heavily influence how we feel, what we do, and even what we believe, it's true. Many people get so caught up in their thoughts that they actually believe they are those thoughts. Nope! We are not our thoughts. The fact that we can talk about our thoughts proves there's more to us than what we think.

You Are Not Your Roles

"I am a mother." "I am a teacher." "I am a partner." We tend to focus heavily on our roles. This can be especially tough after a breakup, when suddenly "I'm a wife" or "I'm a girlfriend" no longer applies. Roles help in categorizing our lives, in understanding our responsibilities and fulfilling them. Roles give us a certain simplicity to life. But roles change, don't they? As you are going through this breakup, you're surely feeling that. But remember: you are not your roles.

You Are Not What You Do

Many of us get caught up in what we do—or don't do. We take on the identity of a "successful businesswoman" or "a runner" or "an animal lover." For instance, I am a psychologist. It is heavily ingrained in the way I think and act in the world. I have a strong curiosity to comprehend how we humans work, and I have a natural ability to understand and have compassion for others. These things make me good at what I do, but do they define who I am? No. They're just part of how I express myself in this world.

Who You Are

So if none of these things we think with our head or feel with our heart gives us the full picture, then I ask again, "Who are you, *really?*"

This is a question that can only be answered with the soul—with that deeper part of you, that timeless, ingrained knowledge that you are more than meets the eye. As we work to discover your sense of self-worth, you will feel that bigger, eternal part of yourself—and you will know that your potential is endless and your ability to love is immense. You will come to know the real you—not the you everyone sees or hears or thinks they know, but the you that was created for a great purpose. You will begin to see yourself as God sees you, and that is true self-worth.

Integrating the Mind, Heart, and Soul of Who You Are

As we move into how to build unwavering self-esteem, it can help to see who you *think* and *feel* you are, because the more you see of yourself and how you are in the world, the more you can integrate it with who you *really* are, deep in your soul.

That's what we're working toward here—to hear what you're saying in your head and feel what you're feeling in your heart, and then bring them in line with what you experience in your soul. Are these three areas saying the same thing about who *you* are? Do you like what you are hearing?

Bottom Line...

- "Who am I?" is a huge question, and we tend to answer it with our head or our heart.

- We are not our roles, our feelings, our thoughts, or behaviors. However, these things can help us understand ourselves better when integrated with the truth from our soul.

Tool: Ask Yourself, "Who Am I?"

- ♥ **Head:** The Who Am I? List. Grab your journal and sit in a quiet space. Create a Who Am I? list. Write out all the titles and roles and qualities your head tells you that you are. Don't judge, just list.

- ♥ **Heart:** The I Am Exercise. Sit in front of a mirror. Breathe. Using the list of words that follows, slowly say, "I am," followed by each trait on the list. Circle those that hold any kind of emotion for you. If one bothers you, circle it. If you know one to be true, circle it. This is a great way for your heart to feel some of who and how you are without the head getting in the way.

Kind	Adventurous	Selfless
Angry	Jealous	Compassionate
Grateful	Giving	Hardhearted
Unhealthy	Greedy	Strong
Lost	Mean	Judgmental
Hopeful	Honest	Loving
Disturbed	Talented	Tired
Faithful	Happy	Joyful
Crazy	Patient	Negative
Sexy	Scared	Wise
Studious	Growing	Brave
Courageous	Flamboyant	Passionate
Selfish	Safe	Dramatic
Flawed	Extroverted	Average
Perfectionistic	Quiet	Emotional
Cruel	Smart	Grounded
Introverted	Committed	Gifted
Open	Relaxed	Helpful
Close-minded	Poised	Unpredictable
Solid	Dishonest	Responsible
Hurtful	Loved	Messy
Weak	A dreamer	Conscientious
Simple	Loud	Shining
Sick	Healthy	Stressed
Picky	Imperfect	Sad
Unlovable	Friendly	Peaceful
Complex	Shy	Lame
Caring	Creative	Fearful
Intelligent	Lazy	Exceptional

♥ **Soul:** Spirit Meditation. Sit in a quiet, comfortable place. Start with ten slow, deep breaths. Next, focus on the insides of your feet. What does it feel like *inside* your feet and toes? Move up into your legs. What does it feel like *inside* your legs? What does it feel like inside your belly, chest, and back? Continue to breathe deeply and focus on the inside of your shoulders and arms. What does it feel like? Focus on your neck, then chin, cheeks, and face. What do these feel like? What does it feel like behind your eyes and inside your brain and ears? Take three slow, deep breaths. Now, notice the sensation in your body. It might feel like a tingling or an energy running through you. If you struggle, focus on your hands, where it's easiest to feel. *This is your spirit.* Feel the vastness of your spirit and how it has no beginning and no end. Continue breathing and feeling your spirit until you're ready to open your eyes. Write down what you experienced. Could you feel how you are so much more than meets the eye? You can also watch a demonstration of this exercise online at http://www.whoamiwithoutyou.com.

23 Shift from "self-esteem" to "self-worth."

A person's worth is contingent upon who he is,
not upon what he does, or how much he has.
The worth of a person, or a thing, or an idea,
is in being, not in doing, not in having.

—Alice Mary Hilton

Over the years, it's become clear that nearly everyone who walks through my private practice door is really dealing with the same core issue: poor self-esteem. Whether struggling through a breakup, divorce, depression, anxiety, addiction, parenting challenge, or even life stress, when we get to the core of the issue, it almost always has to do with some false feeling or belief about oneself.

This has had me wondering over the years: *Why is it so hard to feel self-esteem?* Certainly, it's a hot topic; a Google search will return around 60 million results! There is plenty of advice out there on how to "understand," "evaluate," and "improve" self-esteem, on teaching self-esteem to kids, teens, women, and couples. As one major psychology site writes, "Perhaps no other self-help topic has spawned so much advice and so many (often conflicting) theories" (*Psychology Today* 2013). I agree.

The Problem with "Self-Esteem"

So if we know self-esteem is a problem, and we know there's plenty out there to teach us how to overcome the problem, why does it so strongly persist? I see people all the time who have read these books and articles and have *really* tried; yet they still don't *feel* self-esteem. They don't *believe* they're of worth. Could the fact that so many people are struggling to feel self-esteem be a clue that something isn't right?

I can tell you, something *isn't* right. In fact, I've come to see that the entire concept of "self-esteem" is not right. And that is the real problem: the very thing we are trying to pursue is all wrong.

You may be thinking, "But wait! Aren't we *supposed* to pursue self-esteem? Isn't it the way we learn to love ourselves? Isn't that what this book is about?" Certainly, we've been taught to pursue self-esteem, and we are working on self-esteem in this book. But what we've been taught is *wrong*; the pursuit of self-esteem alone is a myth, and we need a paradigm shift to get it right. Allow me to explain.

Defining Self-Esteem

First, let's define "self-esteem." Some common definitions I have gathered over the years include:

1. Positive or negative evaluations of the self, and how one feels about one's self

2. The totality of beliefs, emotions, thoughts, and power of conviction about oneself

3. One's overall evaluation or appraisal of his or her own worth

Reading these definitions, it's easy to see that "self-esteem," while it *sounds* like a valuable and worthy goal, is based on one's own thinking, perceptions, and emotions related to one's performance and behavior. That's where the problem lies.

Why the Pursuit of Self-Esteem Is a Myth

As we discussed in the previous chapter, we can never know who we really are or build a strong sense of self-worth if we base it on things that are bound to change. The following reasons demonstrate why the pursuit of self-esteem is a myth:

- **Self-esteem is based on what we do and how we behave.** If our worth is based on our performance or behavior, then we are bound to feel poorly about ourselves when our performance or behavior drops; and it *will* drop—that's human nature. We are *more* than what we do and how we behave.

- **Self-esteem is based on how we feel about ourselves.** As we already discussed, basing our worth on our emotions can never succeed, because emotions are fickle and often false. We can *feel* like "bad" people when that's absolutely not the case. We are *more* than how we feel about ourselves.

- **Self-esteem is based on what we think about ourselves.** We've already made this case in previous chapters. We are definitely *more* than what we think about ourselves.

- **Self-esteem is based on how we're doing compared to others.** Instead of evaluating ourselves on how we're doing compared to our *own* potential, which is healthy, pursuing self-esteem teaches us to compare ourselves to *others*. It's fine to compare to others at times *if* it helps us see something to work on or inspires us to grow, but usually comparing ourselves to others just makes us feel worse. No matter how great we are at any given thing, there will always be somebody smarter, faster, skinnier, braver, kinder, and more talented. That's when the identity crisis hits. We *absolutely* cannot base our own worth on what others do or don't do.

- **Self-esteem is based entirely on judgments, whether from others or from ourselves.** Nothing good can come of that. We are certainly *more* than we or anyone else judges us to be.

If Not Self-Esteem, Then What?

I hope it's easy to understand now why self-esteem is so hard to obtain—why, like a sand castle, it's so hard to maintain and so easy to destroy. It looks beautiful and sturdy, but one shift of the wind or tide and down it crashes.

Yes, we need to feel good about ourselves. Yes, we need to love ourselves. Yes, we deserve both of these, but when we base our worth and love for ourselves on anything external, we will *always* fail.

Bottom Line...

- The pursuit of self-esteem alone is a myth because it is based on external factors that are bound to change.

- Instead, we need a paradigm shift: we need to uncover, discover and build self-*worth*.

Tool: Move from Self-Esteem to Self-Worth

♥ Think of an instance when someone else was wrong about your value. Think of a time when you underestimated your own value. Write about how these instances made you feel. How did you know that you or the other person were wrong? Keep this as proof in the future that there is more to you than your own or others' evaluations.

♥ Search for proof that you're more than how you think, feel, behave, or who you are judged to be. Keep a growing list of evidence to support what you are *not* and who you truly are.

24 Learn about the Pyramid of Self-Worth.

Self-worth comes from one thing—
thinking that you are worthy.

—Dr. Wayne Dyer

How do you help someone *feel* lovable if she doesn't *believe* she is? I've been asking this question for years. First, I tried teaching my clients the skills of cognitive behavioral therapy, like we learned in chapters 13 through 17. This helped—to some degree. It targeted the thoughts and feelings that lead to poor self-worth, and it created more realistic and hopeful beliefs. However, I continued to hear, "I know you're *telling* me I am of value, and I can even tell it to myself because I know, in my head, it should be true—but I don't *feel* it." This fueled me to find an answer. It led me to create what I call the Pyramid of Self-Worth.

Understanding the Pyramid of Self-Worth

The Pyramid of Self-Worth is a theory and method I've developed for how to teach people to experience and feel their true worth. The basic premise is that, instead of creating our sense of self by what we think, or how we look, or what we do—self-esteem—we must first build our sense of self-worth by going deep inside, into our soul. As we do this, we build self-worth not by creating a "persona" or by indulging our ego, or false self. Rather, we get to know who we already are and who we have the potential to become.

Working through the Pyramid of Self-Worth begins with *self-awareness*, to see all of who we are; then moves to *self-acceptance*, to accept what we see; and finally to *self-love*, or learning to cherish and appreciate who we are and who we have the potential to become. This leads to a strong sense of *self-worth* and the experience of unwavering self-esteem. (To see the Pyramid of Self-Worth in graphic form, visit http://www.whoamiwithoutyou.com.) We will discuss each of these in the chapters to follow, but, for now, allow me to give you a brief introduction.

Self-Awareness

Self-awareness involves a willingness to see all parts of who you are—your strengths and weaknesses, traits and states, your relationships, values, and what this breakup has meant to you. Before you can *accept* who you are, you have to see yourself.

Self-Acceptance

After you see the parts of who you are, it's time to accept them. Some struggle to accept strengths, while others fail to embrace weakness. Self-acceptance is central to experiencing self-worth.

Self-Love

Finally, it's time to love all you've seen and accepted. Self-love involves self-compassion, kindness, giving and receiving love to others, and self-care. It's the final layer that unlocks the full experience of self-worth. It is a crucial element of healing and learning to love and be loved again.

Self-Worth

Through practicing self-awareness, self-acceptance, and self-love, we begin to feel our true worth. We begin to understand our divine potential and feel God's love for us. Cultivating self-worth is a life-long process, one we will explore in greater detail in the chapters to come.

Bottom Line...

- You can learn to feel and experience your true worth and potential.

- The Pyramid of Self-Worth can show you how.

Tool: Prepare to Work the Pyramid of Self-Worth

- ♥ Can you relate to this statement: "I know you're *telling* me I am important and of value; I know, in my head, it should be true; but I don't *feel* it"? If so, write out the ways in which you can relate. If not, why not? What stands in your way of feeling self-worth? Write about this in your journal.

- ♥ Do you ever struggle with self-awareness? Self-acceptance? Self-love? In what ways do you struggle? What strengths do you possess that might help you work through the Pyramid of Self-Worth? Write it down.

25 Rebuilding, step 1: Practice self-awareness.

Your visions will become clear only when you can look into your own heart. Who looks outside, dreams; who looks inside, awakes.

—Carl Jung

Let's start with the first phase of the Pyramid of Self-Worth: self-awareness. For our purposes, "self-awareness" means the ability to allow yourself to *see* yourself—including the good, the not-so-good, and, yes, even the ugly.

For many, self-awareness is difficult. Why is this so? I think it all boils down to fear. Fear of seeing something really ugly if we dig too deep. Fear of feeling worse about ourselves because of what we see. Fear that once we see we'll have to make change—because making change can be scary.

Self-Awareness Requires Courage

I believe self-awareness requires courage. You may be saying, "But I'm not courageous." Yes, you are. Look at all you've been through. It takes courage to pick up this book and read it. It takes courage to get honest with yourself about your breakup, and how and who you are. It takes courage to do the exercises in this book, to desire change, and to work on that desire. Yes, *you* are courageous, and that is great news because self-awareness requires courage.

Self-Awareness Dispels Fear

Sure, it might be tough to see what we uncover at first, but as we courageously take a deep breath, open up our heart, and step inside, we find the truth; and, as the Bible says, "the truth shall set you free" (John 8:32)—in this case, free of fear. It's easy to fear the monsters hiding in the closet; seeing them in the light is what takes the fear away. The more of us we expose to the light, the less there is to fear, because the more we know.

Self-Awareness Can Be Exciting

Yes, it can be hard to want to see who we really are, but it can also be exhilarating. We not only see the "negatives," we also get to discover our strengths. We have both, after all: strengths *and* weaknesses. We tend to rule these as either "positive" or "negative," but actually these traits, by nature, are neutral. It's only in how we use them that they become positive or negative.

For example, a woman may feel like her "temper" is negative, and when she's yelling at her ex out of frustration, it is. However, when she uses that energy to protect herself from being mistreated, then it's a strength, a positive. As we work on the negatives, they may become positives. That's why self-awareness is such an exciting endeavor: it opens the door for lifelong progress.

Bottom Line...

- Self-awareness requires courage; it can be difficult because we fear seeing the good, bad, and ugly of who we are.

- Self-awareness leads to less fear and greater peace. It has the potential to be exhilarating, once we open up and get started.

Tool: Practice Self-Awareness

♥ Investigate. Imagine you're a detective out to explore and gather the facts about who you are. Start with two lists: I Am and I Am Not.

♥ Create your I Am list. You've been examining your thoughts, feelings, and behaviors for a while now. Ask yourself, "What facts have I uncovered about myself so far?" Have you seen some of your strengths and weaknesses play out as you've been navigating this breakup? Can you admit to some less-desirable traits you have witnessed? What about more-desirable traits? Write these down.

♥ Create your I Am Not list. This can help you remember who you are not. Include things like, "I am not my negative feelings about my ex," or "I am not how I behaved the other day." The more you uncover, the more you keep adding to your lists.

26 Ask yourself, "How am I?"

> **Behavior is what a [person] does, not what he [or she] thinks, feels, or believes.**
>
> **—Anonymous**

As we continue to discover the answer to "*Who* am I?" it's important to ask another question: "*How* am I?" This doesn't refer to how you feel. Instead, we're talking about how you behave, how you are in the world.

Open to the Truth of How You Are

What do you like and dislike about how you interact with others or how you are in your relationships? How do people perceive you? What would you like to change or improve about these things? Understanding *how* you are in the world is great information for helping you see and break old, unhealthy patterns and discover the true you. It's another way we can practice self-awareness.

What I'm asking you to do here is the epitome of vulnerability—going back to look at your relationships with an honest, open heart—but vulnerability is the only lens through which you can see yourself clearly. You must see the truth of how you behave with others in order to understand what is working and what needs work. We're not trying to see who was at fault for the breakup. We're trying to help you discover more elements of who you have been in the past and who you desire to become.

Listen to Others

Sometimes other people tell us things they admire in us or things they really don't like. Do we listen? Hopefully we do. These things can give us great insight. They can show us things we've never seen in ourselves. They can provide an outside perspective on how we come across to other people.

I don't want to confuse you, though. I'm not saying we *must* listen to what others say about us. I'm not saying we should try to be who others want us to be. No. I've already made the point that we are so much more than what other people think. What I'm saying is it can be quite helpful to *consider* the things other people see in us. Do we see them, too? If so, perhaps we should take their words to heart. If not, well, perhaps they are wrong. Either way, it doesn't hurt to listen—to analyze what they say and then decide for ourselves what we believe. And it just might help us see something we otherwise wouldn't have seen.

How Are You?

So, how are you with people? With your friends, neighbors, family members? With your coworkers, church, or community members? With your intimate relationships? Do you tend to get lost in other people? Or do you tend to dominate relationships? Do you always put others' needs first? Or are you more self-focused, forsaking others' needs for your own?

There are all kinds of attributes we only see through the lens of our relationships. I like to say that if I lived alone on a desert island,

I would be a pretty amazing human being. I would never hurt anybody with my words, or be pushed beyond my limits by, say, a screaming child (or two, or three). I would never unintentionally "lose it" with someone I care about. I would feel like a good person. But I would also be *all alone*. No one to love. No one to celebrate with. No one to push me to be better. We need other people. Looking through the lens of our relationships can give us incredible insight into whom we have the potential to become.

Bottom Line...

- Part of discovering who you are is taking an honest look at *how* you are—how you behave in your relationships and in the world.

- Open yourself up and listen to what others say. Later, you can weigh the evidence you've gathered and decide for yourself who you will be.

Tool: Discover *How* You Are

- ♥ Talk with people who know and love you best. Ask how they perceive you. Be open, and discuss.

- ♥ Warning: This exercise is not for the faint of heart. Select three close friends. Ask them to list the three things they admire most about you and the three things they admire least. It's hard to hear how others perceive us, but it's a great way to practice self-awareness and make positive change.

27 See the not-so-good.

She hoped to be wise and reasonable in time;
but alas! Alas! She must confess to herself
that she was not wise yet.

—Jane Austen

What are your weaknesses? We all have them. It's no secret. They tend to shout rather obnoxiously when you go through a breakup or divorce, don't they? The trouble is that most of us tend to either under- or overestimate our weaknesses—and our strengths. Getting real about strengths and weaknesses opens us up and, eventually, helps us to accept and even change them.

Get to Know Your Shadow

Do you have a "dark side?" If you say "no," I don't believe you. We all have a dark side, and I don't mean an evil side, like Darth Vader. I mean we all have a side we want to hide, a side we struggle to accept. Some of us may have exposed parts—or perhaps, with work, all—of this dark side. Others have yet to begin.

Jungian psychology calls this our "shadow." I love that term because it gives such a perfect visual. Your shadow refers to all the things you hide, push away, or run from, the things you deny and wish you didn't see in yourself. The more we run from or deny the shadow, however, the bigger and scarier it becomes. It's only in exposing shadows to the light that they disappear. As we face our weakness, our darkness, we take the shadow's power away.

The Truth About Weakness

What are you not so great at? Are those things easy to identify, or do you struggle to admit where you struggle? For years, I've worked on exposing my shadow side, and some things I can easily admit. If someone were to tell me that I'm not a great gardener, I would agree. I know that I can't remember to water my house plants, let alone a yard. I have friends who are great gardeners—master gardeners even. It is *their* strength. It's not mine. I can also finally admit that I am highly sensitive to physical and emotional stimulation. I can't seem to be nice when I've had no sleep, I react far too strongly to criticism, I'm overemotional, and I prefer being alone to being in a crowd. There are plenty of things I'm still working to accept, but uncovering my weaknesses helps me to understand myself. This process helps us *accept* ourselves, and acceptance is a requisite for self-worth and unwavering self-esteem.

When examining your weaknesses, or shadow, there are a couple things to keep in mind.

1. **Our strengths and weaknesses change with life's circumstances.** For example, as you go through your breakup you might feel weak in setting boundaries with your ex, yet prior to your breakup you felt like boundaries weren't an issue for you. That's just the way it goes. We're given circumstances that make us grow in new ways, develop new strengths, and overcome old weaknesses.

2. **Accepting weaknesses allows us to improve and grow.** As we see a weakness, we can choose to accept it—"That's just how I am, and I like me"—or we can set goals to improve. With work, someday our weaknesses may transform into one of our strengths.

Bottom Line...

- We all have weaknesses, or what can be called a "shadow."

- As we learn to see, and eventually accept, our shadow, we can improve our self-worth and grow.

Tool: See Your Shadow

- ❤ Create a Weaknesses list. Go ahead. Just write your weaknesses down, and keep adding to this list as you uncover more. It's good to expose your weaknesses, to get them onto paper and see that they're nothing more than a word or trait or emotion that you can either continue to fight with, accept, or change.

- ❤ Try this Shadow exercise. Have your journal or your Weaknesses list handy. Then sit quietly and take five slow, deep breaths. Imagine you're entering a dark basement. This basement holds your shadow. As you walk down the stairs, you feel nervous, afraid of what you might find. There are cobwebs and blackness. You see no light. But you've brought a flashlight, and as you turn it on you begin to feel hope, knowing your shadow cannot exist in the presence of the light. Slowly shine your light into each nook and corner as you discover the darker parts of yourself. Remember, you can always turn the light brighter, or retreat back upstairs if it gets to be too much. Continue to breathe as you explore all parts of your shadow, reminding yourself that *you* are *not* these things. You are the one shining the light and discovering the truth. You are the one emerging when you're finished, with a new sense of courage and hope. Open your eyes. Write down what you uncovered. (For an audio download of this exercise, please visit http://www.whoamiwithoutyou.com.)

28 See the good.

A confident person doesn't concentrate or focus on their weaknesses—they maximize their strengths.

—Joyce Meyer

What are your strengths? Can you name them easily, or do you fight to think up even one? Self-awareness involves seeing the "good," not just the "bad and the ugly." Can you see the good in you?

What Are "Strengths"?

What makes something a strength, anyway? There are all kinds of positive traits human beings may exhibit—compassion, discipline, responsibility, optimism, hope, gratitude, kindness, courage, creativity, inspiration, motivation, joy. The list is endless, but what makes these traits "positive"? Are traits inherently "good" or "bad"? We like to think they are, but they're not. Traits are neutral. It's what we *do* with the traits that make them positive or negative, good or bad.

For example, surely being responsible is a good thing, right? Well, what about the woman who is so "responsible"—getting everything done—that she forgets to slow down and enjoy her life? Or the person who's so outwardly joyful all the time that others don't feel comfortable talking to her about "real life" problems? Or the woman who is so optimistic that she continues to believe her relationship is going to make it, even when it's clear things are coming to an end?

See? Too much of a good thing is still too much, even when it comes to personality traits. Traits are neutral. It's what we do with them that turns them into strengths or weaknesses.

A strength, then, instead of being positive, is a trait we use in particularly helpful ways. It's something we're good at. Like muscles, the more we use them the stronger our strengths (and our weaknesses) become. And we don't have to feel the strength of our strengths in order to have them. We're all better at some things than others. You might be a great listener, a talented actor, incredibly organized, highly intelligent, good with directions, great at creating computer code, physically fit, emotionally strong, or many other things. But none of us is good at *all* things.

See Your Strengths

Many women seem to have a harder time seeing their strengths than their weaknesses. Especially during trials, it can feel as if we have *no* strengths. Some facts on strengths:

- **You do yourself no favors by ignoring or denying your strengths.** You have them. So why hide them? Once again, the likely answer is fear. We fear what we do not embrace and accept in ourselves. Better to accept it now: You have a light. You are fabulous. You might not know it yet. You might not feel it yet. But trust me, you do and you are.

- **Owning your strengths allows you to bring passion and purpose to your life.** Do you want a life of purpose and meaning? Own your strengths. When we know we're good at something, we seek more of that in our life. This can increase our passion and even help us discover our life's purpose.

- **Working from your signature strengths is one of the surest ways to increase joy and happiness in your life.** Too often we fail to take the time to search these strengths out and creatively seek ways to use them in our daily pursuits. But it's worth the effort; research shows that using our strengths in a new way each day is a sure path to joy (Seligman et al. 2005).

It's time to let yourself see the light that's uniquely yours. It's time to own it. Then it's time to let that light shine.

Bottom Line…

- Traits are neither inherently "good" nor "bad"; it's what we do with them that makes them strengths or weaknesses.

- Strengths, like muscles, can be strengthened. You can do this by working on them and sharing them with the world.

Tool: Strengthen Your Strengths

- ♥ Create a Strengths list. What strengths do you see in yourself? What do other people see and say about you? Create a list of all your strengths. Add to it as you discover new ones.

- ♥ Compare your Strengths and Weaknesses lists. Is one longer than the other? Why? Are you being honest and letting yourself own your strengths and weaknesses alike? Do you need practice seeing your strengths or weaknesses?

- ♥ Choose one strength to strengthen and one weakness to improve. Start small. Just one by one. Give yourself time, and you will grow.

29 Rebuilding, step 2: Practice self-acceptance.

> Because one believes in oneself, one doesn't try to
> convince others. Because one is content with oneself,
> one doesn't need others' approval. Because one
> accepts oneself, the whole world accepts him or her.
>
> **—Lao-tzu**

Once you can see who and how you are in this world, it's time to work on accepting it. This can be one of the hardest steps, I know, but it's also one of the most important. It's important because until you learn to accept yourself you will never feel good enough. You will continue to battle, holding yourself back and preventing love. You don't want that, do you?

What Is Self-Acceptance?

In chapter 6, we talked about "accepting what *is*." In this case, what *is* is you. At this moment, you are how you are. You feel what you feel. You've done what you've done. Your circumstances are your circumstances, and all of these must be accepted. You don't have to suddenly like what you've seen; you simply have to accept that it *is*.

Some common definitions of the word "accept" include: to come to terms with something; to process something; to receive for review. Accepting yourself, therefore, means you are ready to come to terms with yourself. Self-acceptance is the process of being where we are long enough to appreciate where we have been and where we are headed. It is an end to the pursuit of self-esteem and "trying to be something or someone." Self-acceptance allows us, instead, to discover who we really are.

Self-Acceptance Is Hard

I used to sit with clients after we had been working on self-awareness for a while, and ask, "Can you accept the things you've discovered about yourself now?" I'm not sure why I expected that in *seeing* who they really are they would naturally then *accept* who they are. Many struggled to accept their strengths: "I see it, but I don't know how to accept it." "People always say I'm a giving person, but I don't feel like I give enough." I wondered how to help someone feel something he or she had never felt before.

Psychologist Carl Jung once said, "The most terrifying thing is to accept oneself completely." Why is this so? What is so terrifying about seeing and accepting the truth? This question can only be answered individually, but there are a few things that I think make self-acceptance hard:

- **We aren't sure *how* to accept ourselves.** We fight and fight, trying to protect ourselves, without even knowing we're doing it. Instead, we must learn to give up the fight and submit to self-acceptance. No one is perfect. Have compassion for yourself.

- **Self-acceptance requires us to change,** and we've already discussed how difficult change can be.

- **We may fear that in accepting how we are, we agree with it or think that we will never change.** That's not the case.

As we discussed before, accepting is not the same as agreeing with or liking something. It simply means we give up the fight about how things already are.

Self-Acceptance Is Possible

Hard as it may seem, however, self-acceptance is possible, and, if we work on it, probable. Understanding the following things can help you as you work toward self-acceptance:

- **Self-acceptance, at its core, is a choice.** Only *I* can choose to accept myself, and when I choose not to accept myself, only *I* am standing in my way. Do you understand the power of what I'm saying? Self-acceptance is our choice. It is up to us.

- **Self-acceptance is unconditional.** It's not that we accept what we like and reject what we do not. That's what gets us into self-esteem trouble in the first place. No. Self-acceptance is an all-in deal. It means you are willing to let go of judgment and let things be as they are. It doesn't mean you're giving up or giving in. In fact, the opposite is true. As you accept all things unconditionally, you open the door to true personal growth and development.

- **Self-acceptance is a process.** Some are able to put all the pieces together and say, "This is how I am, and I accept me," while others struggle to accept even the smallest piece. For most, self-acceptance is a day-by-day, moment-by-moment process. I've found that it's most helpful to begin by accepting the small pieces as they come. It can feel less overwhelming this way, yet the process still leads toward the goal of complete self-acceptance. Some things will be difficult to accept, but, with time and work, the process of self-acceptance cleanses and frees us to simply be who we are.

Bottom Line...

- After we *see* who and how we are, we must work to accept it.

- Self-acceptance is a lifelong process that can and will set us free.

Tool: Prepare for Self-Acceptance

♥ Ask yourself the following questions honestly: "What is most authentic about me?" "What is my greatest fear?" "What do I most fear that people will find out about me?" "What do I wish people knew about me?" "When do I feel most truly myself?" "Who am I without my mask, my persona, my ego?" Write your responses in your journal.

30 Learn how to accept yourself.

My definition of success is total self-acceptance.

—Viktor Frankl

That's the big question, isn't it: "*How* do I accept myself?" First, it's important to understand some basic principles of self-acceptance. Next, I've found it helps to use exercises; having something to *do* seems to take the pressure off. Yes, instead of feeling like you have to sit and wait to discover self-acceptance, you can actively work on it.

Basic Principles for Self-Acceptance

True, self-acceptance takes work and dedication, but all that work and dedication will get you nowhere unless you abide by a few basic principles.

1. **Commit to personal growth.** Self-acceptance doesn't happen by saying, "I accept how I am, and I'll always be this way." It happens by being able to say, "I accept how I am now, and I see my potential to become even better." Then, it's about *doing* it. You must commit to developing yourself to your fullest potential in order to make that happen.

2. **Abandon self-defeating behaviors.** It's hard to accept behaviors that you know are unhealthy. Behaviors like

addictions, self-harm, and any other action you know is harmful will only prevent self-acceptance. Work on letting them go in order to be free of the pain of self-defeat. Seek counseling for help as needed.

3. **Change your beliefs.** Most of the "fighting" we do against self-acceptance is all in our head. Go back to chapters 13 through 17 and continue to create new, healthy schema about yourself until you can actually accept them as true.

Self-Acceptance Exercise

Take out your Strengths and Weaknesses lists (chapters 27 and 28), and refer to the circled words in the I Am exercise (chapter 22). If you haven't yet completed these exercises, go and do so now.

As you did these exercises, you likely noticed that some things were easy to accept: "I am emotional. Yep, I certainly am." Others were not so easy: "I am…mean… I guess I can come off that way, but I don't want to be mean." Often, the traits we despise are those we have the most trouble accepting. Or we may struggle to accept the positives: "I wish I were talented. People tell me I am, but I really don't feel that way."

Now, go back through the traits on these lists. Say each out loud and see how it feels. "I am creative," "I am stubborn," "I am a hard worker," "I am jealous." Those that are easy to own are those you have accepted. Those that feel hard to swallow will need more work.

As you go throughout your days and weeks, be mindful of those parts of you that you struggle to accept. Acceptance comes moment by moment, with love. When an unwanted weakness rears its ugly head, take a deep breath and repeat, "I see this, and I accept that it *is*." When a strength shows up, do the exact same thing.

Tips for Working on Self-Acceptance

Keep these pointers in mind:

- **Self-acceptance takes time.** Some parts of you may take weeks or even months to fully accept. As you continue to make self-acceptance a daily focus, you will eventually be able to let go and accept all of you.

- **Your family history can influence how self-accepting you are.** We learn patterns of self-acceptance from our family. Maybe your parents always helped you identify and accept your strengths and weaknesses. Maybe you learned to hide weakness or that it was not acceptable to show strength. Be mindful of the impact your family history might have had on you.

- **Accepting yourself doesn't mean that you think you are the best or the worst.** Saying, "I am a singer," doesn't translate to "I am the best singer ever!" It's simply saying that you see and acknowledge that part of who you are. If singing is a part of your life, then you're a singer. Accept it.

- **Self-acceptance is a lifelong process,** because you will always be learning new things about yourself. Each day, each moment, you have the option to accept these things and to accept yourself. The more you work on it, the more of a strength self-acceptance will become for you.

Bottom Line...

- Self-acceptance requires work—and a willingness to do that work.

- Part of self-acceptance is the choice to let go of old beliefs and behaviors, and commit to personal growth.

Tool: Practice Self-Acceptance

♥ Do the Self-Acceptance exercise presented in this chapter. How did it feel to do this exercise? Which traits do you continue to struggle with? Write about them in your journal. What would it take for you to let go and accept them?

♥ Imagine you could accept every part of who and how you are. What would that feel like? How would it impact you? Your relationships? Your world? Write down your feelings.

31 Stop the blame game and own your "stuff."

Blame ties us to the past and makes our mind smaller.
It dampens our delight and limits our possibilities.

—Sakyong Mipham

Blame is easy when you're going through a breakup or divorce. I have no doubt we could talk for hours about all the things your ex has done to you. Yet blame does nothing except keep you in a place of anger, pain, and nonacceptance. Part of self-acceptance is accepting what you've been through—accepting your ex's part in things, taking responsibility for your part in things, owning your "stuff."

The Truth About Blame, Pain, and Suffering

Sometimes other people do hurt us—physically, emotionally, spiritually. Abuse is real, and I certainly would never diminish those experiences. Some of us had parents who taught us we were worthless. Some had teachers who pointed out every mistake and helped create this flawed belief system we have about ourselves today. Some had intimate partners who were controlling, full of spite, and who reminded us that we could never be good enough. Yes, other people definitely can hurt us. Only they are at fault for the damage they have done.

Additionally, we damage ourselves. When we hold on to the past—to anger, heartache, or blame—we reinjure ourselves over and over. As author Haruki Murakami said, "Pain is inevitable. Suffering is optional." Others may cause us pain, but only we allow suffering.

How to Let Go of Blame and Accept

So what are we to do? Work to let go of blame. Letting go of blame frees us. It is part of the path to self-acceptance. Here are five suggestions for how:

1. **Accept what has happened.** Whether your breakup was amicable or fraught with drama and tension, you must accept what is already done.

2. **Accept the things you *cannot* change.** You have no control over others—what they say or do, or whether "justice" is ever served for how they behaved toward you. No amount of trying to get them to "pay" will ever help you be free. It only hurts and causes you greater suffering. We'll discuss forgiveness in chapter 36. For now, simply accept what you cannot change.

3. **Accept the things you *can* change.** Are there things you regret doing or saying? Have you been holding on to blame? Accept your part in how your relationship has turned out.

4. **Accept that you have the power.** You have the power to let things go. You have the power to give up blame and guilt.

5. **Accept responsibility for your own happiness.** No one else can make you happy. It's all up to you. Accept it. Work to let yourself be happy.

Bottom Line...

- Blame keeps you stuck.

- Accepting what has happened, where you are, and what part you have played is the path to healing and self-worth.

Tool: Own It, Accept It

♥ Without judgment, identify your part in the breakup. Write down what you discover. Look at this as a list of things you can improve.

♥ If you were your therapist, what would you see? In what ways have you blamed others—your ex, family, friends, others—for your own "stuff"? Have you ever blamed others for your sense of self-worth or self-esteem? Be honest. Write out how you feel.

32 Rebuilding, step 3: Practice self-love.

It's not your job to like me...it's *mine*!

—Byron Katie

Self-love is mandatory for self-worth. We must learn to love ourselves completely. It would be easy for me to say, "Go love yourself," and leave it at that. It sounds so simple. But self-love, though simple, is not always easy. Knowing *how* to love ourselves can feel tricky and, sometimes, impossible.

Defining Self-Love

Before we can practice self-love, we must understand what self-love means. First, let's get clear on what self-love is *not*.

Self-Love Is Not...

- **Selfishness.** In fact, selfishness involves very little self-love.

- **Narcissism.** Self-love is neither self-absorption nor self-obsession. It's recognizing your worth and caring about yourself as a result.

- **The opposite of other-love.** Self-love is an important part of loving others. You will never fully love others until you learn to love yourself. You cannot give what you do not already possess.

Self-love has four important elements. When we are able to focus on and practice each of these, we begin to experience self-love and feel our true worth.

Self-Love Is…

- **Self-care: taking care of yourself.** In chapter 5 we discussed how self-care is an absolute necessity. It's also a key element of self-love. Taking care of your body, heart, mind, and spirit all send the same message: "I love myself, so I will take care of myself—body and soul."

- **Self-compassion: developing loving thoughts and feelings about yourself.** It takes into account all of who we are—our good and not so good—and allows us to apply a loving hand when we need it most, then to do the same for others. When we exhibit self-compassion, we choose to think and feel kindly toward ourselves, despite our suffering and mistakes (Neff 2011). It allows us to see that we're just like everyone else—perfectly flawed; it allows us to touch our flawed nature with love.

- **Self-kindness: doing nice things for yourself.** For some, this may mean giving yourself a break by getting someone to watch your kids, or letting yourself go for a hike with friends instead of cleaning the house. It may be as simple as telling yourself you look terrific when you look in the mirror; smiling and shaking off negative feelings when you make a mistake; or reminding yourself, "I am a good person." A good question to ask yourself is, "What would I do to show kindness to someone else?" Then do that for yourself.

- **Letting others love you.** Practice receiving a compliment with a simple "Thank you." When others ask if they can help or serve you, say, "Yes, that would be wonderful." Even returning a smile from a stranger can help the walls come down and the love begin to enter your heart. And listen: *if you think no one loves you, you're wrong.* Letting down your walls and letting love in not only builds healthy relationships that reinforce self-love, it creates a stronger sense of self-worth.

Bottom Line...

- Understanding what self-love is *not* can help you let go of all that holds you back from practicing it.

- Understanding and practicing what self-love *is* opens the door to greater love for and *from* you; it is the door that leads to self-worth.

Tool: Practice Self-Love

♥ Practice self-care, as described above and in chapter 5. Select one aspect of self-care that needs your attention today and do it.

♥ Practice self-compassion. Listen to what you say to yourself throughout each day. Write down everything you hear— the loving and the not-so-loving words. How compassion- ate are you with yourself? What can you do to improve?

♥ Practice self-kindness. Each day, do one kind thing for yourself. It might be a nap or time with friends. It might, and should, include choosing to believe the compassionate thoughts and feelings you are learning to create.

33 Love your physical, emotional, mental, social, and spiritual sides.

To love yourself right now, just as you are, is to give yourself heaven. Don't wait until you die. If you wait, you die now. If you love, you live now.

—Alan Cohen

Unless you care for and love all parts of you, you'll never feel whole, because all sides of you—the physical, emotional, mental, spiritual, and social—are interrelated. Let's examine each and give you some ideas for how to keep all of you in tip-top, well-loved shape.

Physical Self-Love

Physical health is what I call the "base layer of wellness," without which it's tough to feel emotionally, intellectually, spiritually, and socially well. Without a healthy body it's even difficult to tap in to and feel your worth and potential. You must care for your body; make it a top priority.

When you feel pain or illness, or when you're tired or overwhelmed, that is your body saying, "Listen to me! Take care of me!" Physical self-love includes:

- Eating foods that give you energy and health

- Drinking enough water

- Exercising regularly

- Getting enough sleep and resting when your body is worn out

- Managing or treating physical and mental health conditions or illnesses

- Visiting the doctor for regular checkups

- Taking vitamins and supplements that promote health

- Getting a massage or taking a hot bath for sore muscles

- Getting up and going for a walk when you're low in energy

There's no one way to take care of your body, and only you know what your body needs. So listen when your body speaks. Then do what it takes to keep yourself healthy and strong.

Emotional Self-Love

Emotional health includes all you feel and experience day to day. Each of us is unique when it comes to our emotional-health needs. Good physical health promotes good emotional health, but it's not the only solution. Many women, especially after a breakup, feel like they're on an emotional roller coaster—laughing one minute, crying the next. Others are more emotionally shut down, stuffing or ignoring their feelings. No matter how you experience emotions, acknowledging and addressing your emotional needs is an important part of rebuilding self-esteem after a breakup.

You need to feel safe and supported as you seek understanding about who you are, what you need, and how to progress in your emotional growth. This may include:

- Talking or crying with an understanding support person. (Remember that support system we set up in chapter 2?)

- Psychotherapy

- Writing down your experiences and emotions in your journal

- Using your creativity (such as art, writing, dance, etc.) to process emotions and gain understanding

- Participating in online social support forums or social media support pages (see resources below)

Online Divorce/Breakup Support

The "Who Am I Without You?" Breakup & Divorce Support Group on Facebook. Online support and discussion of the principles featured in this book. Visit (http://www.facebook.com/groups/WhoAmIWithoutYou, and request to be added.

Dr. Hibbert's *This Is How We Grow* Personal Growth Group (http://www.DrChristinaHibbert.com). Free online personal growth lessons and group support.

Daily Strength Breakups/Divorce Support Group (http://www.dailystrength.org/c/Breakups-Divorce/support-group). Part of ShareCare, Dr. Oz's health and wellness website. With online discussion and forums specifically for overcoming breakups/divorce.

"The divorce support page of the Internet"—http://DivorceSupport.com. Provides support and information on topics such as family law, child custody, child support, visitation, alimony, and property division.

Mental and Intellectual Self-Love

Mental and intellectual health includes academic learning, but it also includes creativity, life knowledge, and common sense. Some ways you can practice mental and intellectual self-love include:

- Engaging in activities you enjoy that keep your brain active and healthy

- Discussing topics that are of interest to you

- Trying something new

- Reading

- Learning something

- Playing games that require mind focus (like crosswords, sudoku, puzzles)

- Creating something

Social Self-Love

It's natural for some of us to want to isolate in hard times, such as after a relationship ends, but isolation can lead to loneliness, stress, and depression. Instead, seek social interaction that uplifts and encourages you.

- Go to dinner or lunch with a good friend

- Attend a party with people you enjoy

- Go to a concert, play, or sporting event

- Join a club or group

- Sign up for a class or activity that you enjoy

- Spend quality time with family and close friends

You don't have to suddenly go out each night or be at every party to show social love. Just let people in, according to what makes *you* feel healthy and well.

Spiritual Self-Love

Getting in touch or reconnecting with your spirit is one of the best things you can do for your physical, emotional, mental, and social health—after a breakup and always. Those who have a daily spiritual practice often feel more peace and connection in their lives, experience less stress, and have a greater sense of purpose and meaning.

Spirituality can include many different practices. The important thing is to unplug from the busyness of the world and tune in to the softer whisperings that remind us of who we really are.

What helps *you* connect spiritually?

- Prayer

- Meditation

- Religious worship or church

- Music

- Nature

- Reading scripture or sacred texts

Whatever it is, if it is lacking in your life, you'll feel it. Recommit to your spiritual practice and you'll definitely feel that, too.

Bottom Line...

- Part of developing unwavering self-esteem is taking care of yourself—physically, emotionally, mentally, socially, and spiritually.

- As you love all aspects of yourself, you will feel healthier, more loved, and a stronger sense of worth.

Tool: What Do You Need?

- ♥ What are your needs in each of these areas? For instance, physically, do you need more sleep, or better relaxation? Do you have a spiritual practice? Are you engaging in meaningful social interaction? Write down your needs in all of these areas.

- ♥ From your list of needs, select what you consider to be the top three for optimal wellness at this point. Choose one to start working on today. Then move on to the next, and the next, and so on.

34 Rebuilding, step 4: Build on self-worth to reach your fullest potential.

Once the soul awakens, the search begins and you can never go back. From then on, you are inflamed with a special longing that will never again let you linger in the lowlands of complacency and partial fulfillment.

—John O'Donohue

It's time to check in. How are you doing with the Pyramid of Self-Worth? First, have you been doing the exercises? If not, then head back to chapter 24 and get to work. If we want to feel self-worth, we have to do the work.

If you have been doing the exercises, what have you discovered about yourself so far? Can you see some of the good *and* not so good? No matter where you are in this process, if you continue to work through the layers of the Pyramid of Self-Worth, you will eventually feel your worth and see your true potential. That's what step 4 is all about—letting yourself feel and embrace your worth as you widen your focus to see your potential.

Reach Your Fullest Potential

Once we are able to see all parts of us and begin to accept and love them, we are acting from a place of self-worth. This means we finally feel valuable and loved not just by others, but by ourselves and by God. We are starting to experience that sense of unwavering self-esteem. We may still doubt ourselves at times, but we feel more comfortable and confident in who we are.

Just because we are more aware, accepting, and loving of ourselves doesn't mean that we are done with our self-development, however. Of course not. Life is meant to change us—it is meant to help us grow. Even your breakup has a part in helping you grow. In fact, feeling self-worth and self-esteem is merely the first step in becoming who we are meant to be. As we build on self-worth, we can reach our fullest potential.

Who Do You Desire to Become?

Before we can *become* who we want to be, we first must *know* who we want to be. A To Be list can help.

Just like a To Do list helps us focus on the most important things to do each day, our To Be list helps us focus on the most important things to *be*. The following questions can help you develop your To Be list:

1. **Whom do you desire to become?** Do you want to be more compassionate, dedicated, hopeful, or kind? Do you want to develop your natural talents, or learn something new? Do you hope to overcome a challenge or strengthen a particular weakness?

2. **Whom do you *not* want to be?** Perhaps you do not want to end up bitter about your breakup. Or maybe you do not want your children to have lasting consequences because you and your ex can't get along. Knowing what you do *not* want helps you turn it around and discover what you *do* want—in these

examples, you *do* want forgiveness with your ex; you *do* want to give it your all to make and keep the peace.

3. **What would you want your friends and family to say about you at your funeral?** I call this the End of Life visualization. I did this exercise myself a few years back, when I was going through one of my toughest times. I realized that I didn't want my family to say, "Boy, did she sacrifice everything for us." I wanted them to say, "She inspired us, she taught us. She loved deeply and was an example of strength and joy." Answering this question helped me discover the direction that I needed to take, the path toward the person I desired to become. It can do the same for you.

Bottom Line...

- Once you have worked through the Pyramid of Self-Worth, you will begin to *feel* self-worth; you will be ready to build on that self-worth, to reach your fullest potential.

- To know what your potential is and who you desire to become, begin by creating your To Be list.

Tool: Create Your "To Be" List

- ♥ In addition to the questions and exercises above, ask yourself the following and write down your responses: What traits do I admire in others? What traits do I *not* admire? What traits do I seek in my ideal partner? What traits would I need to have in order to *be* an ideal partner?

- ♥ Use all of these things to help you create your To Be list. Add as many traits as you wish. Select one quality to focus on *being* today.

35 Believe in you.

Don't be afraid to be amazing.

—Andy Offutt Irwin

"Believe in yourself." It's cliché, yet so significant. No one concept can make or break us so drastically. In chapter 16, I wrote that you don't have to believe what you are telling yourself, but now that we've worked through the Pyramid of Self-Worth—now that you know who you are and see your potential—it's time to *believe*.

From Affirmations to the Truth

There are countless books, articles, posts, and pins reminding us to think positively about who and how we are. Many of these encourage the use of affirmations to strengthen belief in oneself. I have used affirmations personally and professionally, as well, but there's one thing I've learned about affirmations: they don't always work.

They don't always work because people don't always believe the affirmations. It's one thing to remind yourself of something you already know; it's another to repeat statements such as, "I am beautiful," "I am courageous," "I am over that guy," when really, you're not so sure.

It is only after we've discovered the truth that we can affirm these truths in our mind. This is why we first worked on learning the skills of changing thoughts and beliefs (chapters 13 through 17), and then strengthened our sense of self-worth using the Pyramid of

Self-Worth. Only now that we see the truth may we move from repeating empty affirmations to affirming what we've discovered about who we really are.

How to Believe in Yourself

Here are some things you can do:

- **Make a list of all the things you've learned that encourage you to believe in yourself.** This may include things from your Strengths or Weaknesses lists, from your I Am exercises, or from anything else we have done so far. Be sure to also look back at the alternative responses you created on your Thought Record Part 2.

- **Pick five to ten truths you find most helpful.** Your list might include things like: "I am stronger than I feel," "I am a caring person; it's one of my greatest strengths," "I may feel afraid from time to time, but I face my fears," "I really am beautiful—inside and out." Just go for it—after all your hard work, you deserve to see all the beautiful truths you've discovered.

- **Look through your list and select two or three statements you most need to hear, that most encourage you to believe in *you*.** These are what you're going to affirm to yourself when times get rough. And because they're based on facts *you* uncovered, you can't argue. You already know they're true. You've proven them. They're your *true affirmations*.

- **When hard times come, pull out your true affirmations and remind yourself of what you already know.** For example, if your ex calls, begging for one more chance (again), remind yourself, "I know he's no good for me. I am strong enough to keep my boundaries and say no." Then, do what you know.

Here are other ways to affirm belief in yourself:

- Write helpful quotes and your true affirmations on note cards or sticky notes and stick them on your mirror, nightstand, or desk, so that you see them every day.

- Repeat your true affirmations in your mind or out loud at the beginning and end of each day. You might also set reminders on your mobile device to focus on them throughout the day.

- Carry a card with your true affirmation in your pocket or purse; pull it out and refer to it throughout the day.

- Have someone else write the affirmation for you, if it's easier to believe. I've done this many times for clients. Eventually, my voice becomes their voice. The same might work for you.

Bottom Line...

- A crucial element of unwavering self-esteem is belief in yourself.

- Using the truths you've already uncovered, affirm these truths in hard times; affirm your belief in yourself.

Tool: Discover What You Believe, Then Work on Believing It

- ♥ As described above, revisit your thought records, your Strengths and Weaknesses lists, and any other exercises you've found helpful. Compile a list of what you've learned about yourself so far.

- ♥ Choose two or three positive, *true* messages—your *true affirmations*—to remind yourself of each day. Use the methods above or whatever method works best for you.

36 Forgive.

> To forgive is to set a prisoner free and to
> discover that the prisoner was you.
>
> **—Lewis B. Smedes**

No matter how your relationship ended, you have likely endured painful experiences and hurt feelings—anger, worry, fear, grief. We've learned how to cope with and overcome these feelings. Yet the emotions of a breakup or divorce have only one sure cure: forgiveness. Forgiveness of your ex. Forgiveness of situations, experiences, and other people. Forgiveness of yourself.

Failing to Forgive Destroys Self-Esteem

Forgiveness is much easier once we feel self-worth. That's why we're discussing it now. When we embrace our worth, we're much more likely to see the value and worth of others. This helps us let go of the pain we cause ourselves by failing to forgive. I have long loved the words of the Buddha: "Holding on to anger is like drinking poison and expecting the other person to die." Failing to forgive only hurts *us*. It destroys our self-esteem. It prevents healing.

Shay's husband left her shortly after their first child was born. Becoming a father was too much for him, he said, and so he left them both behind. Shay struggled to find her way as a single mother and eventually ended up in my office, terribly depressed. "How could he do that to us?" she continually asked. Of course, I had great empathy for Shay. I wondered the same thing about her ex and wished I had a good answer. Eventually, it became clear that Shay was stuck on "what he did to me." I gently explained she would never be able to move on until she could find a way to forgive. Even though her ex never asked for forgiveness, and never even acknowledged wrongdoing, Shay soon came to realize that she was letting him poison her by holding on to what he'd done. She was poisoning herself by failing to forgive.

How to Forgive

When it comes to forgiveness, like so many other things in life, the most common question is "How? How do I forgive?" Forgiveness is not easy, but here are some simple steps to get you started:

- **Decide to forgive.** It can take months or even years to feel ready to forgive. Just choose forgiveness, whenever it comes. Once you *decide* to forgive you will be on the path of forgiveness—the path of choosing to love yourself, and to believe in yourself, and to let the past go.

- **Know that forgiveness is a practice and a process.** It is a practice—something you purposefully do over and over. It is also a process—something you may choose to do each moment of each new day.

- **Remember that forgiveness is about compassion.** Just as you must show yourself compassion to feel self-worth, so must you extend compassion to others. Forgiveness requires putting yourself into the other person's shoes. It requires a willingness to offer love and kindness, or at least just understanding, even if you don't get it in return. This may be difficult to do, especially if you've endured abuse. Just remember, extending compassion does not mean you will let yourself be mistreated. It means that *you* choose to treat *others* with forgiveness, which is an act of courage and strength.

- **Forgive yourself.** Feelings of guilt, shame, or self-hatred can prevent self-forgiveness, keeping you stuck in patterns and behaviors of poor self-esteem. However, part of developing self-worth, as we've discussed, is being willing to see and accept *all* parts of you. That includes your deep, dark secrets, your shadow. That includes self-forgiveness. Extend compassion as you lovingly work to admit your mistakes. Forgive what is past, and commit to a brighter future.

Bottom Line...

- Forgiveness is a crucial part of self-esteem after a breakup.

- As you choose to forgive, and then work through the process of forgiveness, you will feel a burden lift. You will be on the path of healing.

Tool: Forgiveness Exercises

- ♥ Visualization exercise: Sit or lie in a comfortable position. Close your eyes. Take three slow, deep breaths. Imagine what your life would be like if you could forgive everyone and everything—including yourself. What would your heart and body feel like? Really feel it. What would your environment look like? Really see it. What would your relationships be like? Really experience it. Stay with this visualization for several minutes, and when you're ready, open your eyes. What did you see? What did you feel? Write it out. Then bring this vision back any time you need to remember to choose forgiveness.

- ♥ Forgiveness practice: Each day, wake up and repeat, "Today I will forgive, then lovingly let go." Moment by moment, choose to forgive.

37 Commit to being better than just "better."

What are you going to do? Everything, is my guess.
It will be a little messy, but embrace the mess. It
will be complicated, but rejoice in the complications.

—Nora Ephron

When we're hurting, all we want is to feel "better." I've learned through my own trials, however, that sometimes "better" isn't good enough. I don't want to only *over*come; I want to *be*come my best self, and I want to flourish.

Overcoming. Becoming. Flourishing.

"Overcoming. Becoming. Flourishing." It's the tagline on my website, and you've probably noticed I've used these three words in parts 1, 2, and 3 of this book, too. That's because I believe we can overcome, become, *and* flourish. This book isn't meant to just help you get *over* your breakup. It's meant to help you discover and become who you really are.

In part 1, we worked on the tools of overcoming. In part 2, we've been working on becoming by using the Pyramid of Self-Worth. We have identified your strengths and weaknesses, worked on accepting and loving yourself. Next, we move on to part 3, which will inspire us to flourish.

Believe You Can Flourish

We mustn't settle for only being "better" when we can learn to experience the emotions of flourishing—joy, peace, gratitude, hope, and love. Why do so many of us fail to believe we can flourish? Perhaps it's because so many of us weren't raised with strong examples of flourishing. Perhaps life has been hard, and we only expect the worst. Perhaps it feels like flourishing would be impossible.

I'm here to tell you it's not. Only you stand in your way of being "better than better." Only you can decide just how *much* better you will become. Work on overcoming your breakup and the challenges of life for as long as it takes, but never settle for "better." Have faith that there are incredible things waiting out there for you.

Bottom Line...

- There is more to life than overcoming challenges—we are meant to become our highest selves; we are destined to flourish.

Tool: Envision "Better Than Better"

- ♥ Better than Better meditation: Sit in a comfortable position, close your eyes, and take three slow, deep breaths. Imagine your future—a future in which you are "better than better." What do you see? What does your family look like? What do your relationships look like? How do you feel? Spend as long as you'd like envisioning your better than better future. Then, when you're ready, open your eyes. Write down what you envisioned.

Part 3

Learning to Love and Be Loved Again

How to Live the Flourishing
Life You Deserve

38 Flourish! Yes, I said, "Flourish!"

Out of suffering have emerged the strongest souls...

—Kahlil Gibran

What does it mean to flourish? According to the field of positive psychology, it means "to live within an optimal range of human functioning, one that connotes goodness, generativity, growth, and resilience" (Frederickson and Losada 2005). Sounds pretty good, doesn't it? It also sounds a lot like overcoming brokenness, experiencing unwavering self-esteem, and living a life of joy and love. When we know who we are, we engage with the world confidently, and when we do this, we flourish.

How to Measure "Flourishing"

A newer branch of psychology, positive psychology does more than simply treat mental illness; it aims to discover and cultivate genius and talent, and to help normal life feel more fulfilling. Flourishing is an area of positive psychology that seeks to help us live according to our highest potential.

How do you know if you are flourishing or not? A good place to start is by asking the four questions positive psychologists use to measure flourishing (Seligman 2009):

1. **How much positive emotion am I creating and receiving in my life?** How much do you focus on feeling happy and well? Do you actively work on this, or do you wait for positive emotions to just show up? Do you practice and feel gratitude? Do you work on developing optimism, patience, kindness, laughter, hope, inspiration, joy, and so on?

2. **How much meaning and purpose do I experience on a daily basis?** Do you look for meaning in your day-to-day interactions? Do you feel a sense of purpose in your life? If not, what might be standing in your way?

3. **How good are my relationships with others?** You might be recovering from the loss of your intimate relationship, but how are your other relationships doing? Do you make relationships a priority? The strength and depth of our relationships directly correlate with our experience of flourishing.

4. **How much mastery, confidence, competence, and achievement do I enjoy in life?** We've just worked on confidence and self-worth for seventeen chapters; so, how confident and competent do you feel at this point? Do you feel worthy of realizing the goals and desires you've set forth for yourself?

Bottom Line...

- "Flourishing" is a term from the field of positive psychology. It means to live in a way that invites goodness, growth, and all kinds of great things into your life.

- The four questions used to measure flourishing can help you evaluate how much flourishing you're already achieving—and help you identify the work needed to achieve even more.

Tool: The Flourishing Assessment

♥ Grab your journal and sit in a quiet, comfortable space. Reread and ponder the four flourishing assessment questions. Write your honest responses, and then write how you feel about what you've discovered.

39 Live in the now.

Realize deeply that the present moment is all you have. Make the now *the primary focus of your life.*

—Eckhart Tolle

After a breakup, when we feel broken and have to work so hard to rebuild our sense of self-worth, it's especially easy to want to live anywhere but right *now*. Life is about what's right in front of us, though. When we miss what's happening now, we miss life. A key element of flourishing—of living a life full of love—is learning to live in the *now*.

The Past Is History

It's common to feel stuck in the past when we're going through any hardship, including a breakup or divorce. We continually remember what we've been through and analyze it, keeping ourselves buried under old emotions. I believe it is a good thing to think about, process, and feel what needs to be felt from the past. Finding meaning and understanding in past experiences can guide our present and future, help us reach our full potential, and help us flourish.

It's getting stuck in the past that causes trouble. When we get stuck in the past, we miss what's right in front of us. We miss opportunities to heal. We miss opportunities to grow. Basically, we miss out on life.

The Future Is a Mystery

After a breakup, we may get stuck in constant planning to try and control the future. Or we may endure incredible anxiety or depression because our minds can only see the negative feelings and experiences to come. We worry and indulge our fears about what *could* happen tomorrow, next week, or years down the road.

Focusing on what might or might not happen and trying to control future events only creates tension and distress. The future is a mystery; we cannot know what will come our way, so there's no use making ourselves miserable over it. The only "control" we have is right now—in the present.

Today Is a Gift—That's Why It's Called the Present

All we really have is *now*, this very moment, and what a gift it is! If we want to overcome the brokenness, if we want to build unwavering self-esteem, if we want a life that flourishes in love, we must learn how to live in the *now*.

In chapter 21, I introduced some mindfulness practices, including deep breathing, focusing on the now, and meditation. All of these show us how to live in the now. Additionally, simple practices like the following can help:

- **Throughout the day remind yourself, "Focus on the now."** Stop, take a deep breath, use all your senses, and take in the world around you.

- **Set a few alarms on your phone or device to go off at different times throughout the day.** Let these remind you to stop and notice the present moment.

- **When you're engaging in an activity, focus all your attention on that activity.** If you're at work, focus completely on each task. If you're making dinner, take in the smells and tastes. If you're with your children, turn off electronics and give them your full attention. Be fully involved in your life each moment of the day.

What to Do When You're Fighting the Now

If you find yourself struggling to be present, don't worry. Noticing the struggle means that you're more aware than you realize. Your awareness of the struggle is, itself, living in the *now*. Here are three suggestions:

1. **Notice the struggle, and let it work itself out.** If you pay attention to the struggle, it brings you back to the now.

2. **FEEL in the present moment.** When challenging moments come, sit still, breathe, and use the techniques we learned in chapter 7 to FEEL the emotions that arise.

3. **Accept what is.** Once again, we must work to accept what *is* (see chapter 6). Accept the challenges, the blessings, and all experiences that come your way. They might feel "good" or "bad" to you; you don't have to like them or want them to happen. You just have to accept that they *are*. Take life moment by moment, noticing each experience and letting it be.

Bottom Line...

- Life is happening right *now*.

- Slow down, pay attention, and take it all in. You don't want to miss it.

Tool: Live in the Now

♥ Do a presence meditation. This exercise will help you focus on the world around you. Once you get the hang of it, use it throughout the day to bring you back to the *now*. Sit comfortably and close your eyes. Take a deep breath in...and out. Continue to breathe, from down in your toes up through your body. What does your body feel like as you breathe? What can you feel on your skin? Continue to breathe gently, as you notice what you smell...and taste. Is there a smell in the air you can practically taste? Do you taste something you recently ate? Continue breathing calmly, as you notice the sound of your own breathing, your own body. Move your attention outward to the sounds around you. Using all the senses available to you, take in the world. Breathe comfortably, and when you're ready, open your eyes. (For an audio download of this meditation, please visit http://www.whoamiwithoutyou.com.)

40 Practice gratitude.

A thankful heart is not only the greatest virtue,
but the parent of all other virtues.

—Cicero

No matter what you've lost through your breakup, you have much to
be grateful for. You have more love in your life than you've likely
realized. You have the potential to feel even greater love. Focusing
on the present allows us to see the good around us, to choose to take
it in and feel grateful for it. Yes, practicing gratitude is one of the
surest paths to a life of love and flourishing.

Go Beyond Feeling Grateful

It's easy to say we're grateful—we're grateful for our family, our job,
our friends, our health. And we mean it. We *are* grateful. We do feel
blessed. But then life intervenes. We experience the breakup, the
loss, the pain, and we stop remembering we're grateful. We stop
feeling like we're blessed. We don't mean to—it's just the way it is.

It doesn't have to be that way. Sure, gratitude can be a state of
emotion—like when we feel overwhelmed with love or catch a beautiful sunset—but we don't have to, and really *shouldn't*, settle for
waiting around to *feel* grateful. We can choose to create the emotions we desire, and gratitude should be at the top of the list.

Benefits of a Gratitude Practice

Leading gratitude researchers Robert Emmons and Charles Shelton have defined gratitude as "a felt sense of wonder, thankfulness, and appreciation for life" (2002). We can cultivate this "wonder, thankfulness, and appreciation of life" by practicing gratitude. The benefits of developing a gratitude practice are well researched and numerous, including physical, emotional, mental, social, and spiritual health benefits. Those who practice gratitude tend to be more optimistic, more forgiving, and, yes, more loving, too (Emmons 2007; Seligman 1990).

Before You Get Started

There are a few things you should know before implementing a gratitude practice:

- The goal is to *actively practice* gratitude, not just wait around to *feel* grateful.

- The best way to make gratitude a habit is to spice it up with different types of gratitude practices.

- It doesn't matter how often you practice gratitude; what matters is that you do it routinely.

9 Ways to Practice Gratitude

Choose one or more of the following, and start practicing gratitude *today*!

1. **Begin a gratitude journal.** Each morning, every night, or once a week, write down three to five things you're grateful for. Try not to repeat items too often—you have more to be grateful for than you realize!

2. **Write a gratitude letter and deliver it in person.** Think of someone who has made a powerful impact on your life. Write him or her a letter of gratitude. Then read the letter in person. You could also mail the letter, but reading it directly to the person is one of the most powerful gratitude practices you can do. It is literally life changing for many people (Seligman 2009).

3. **Incorporate gratitude into exercise or morning routines.** Start with your body, muscles, brain, and go from there. List what you're grateful for in your mind, or say it out loud. For example, each morning, as I warm up for my jog, I do deep-breathing exercises. Then I say a prayer of gratitude, thanking God for as many things as I can think of that day. If I'm outside, I notice the trees, weather, and people waving hello. This helps me smile through my exercise and gets my day started right. Each day is something new.

4. **Post words, photos, and objects of gratitude in your home.** Place the items where you'll see them. Then let them remind you to stop and be grateful. I have a wooden cutout of the word "Gratitude" in my kitchen, and the words "Begin each day with a grateful heart" are framed in my office. What motivates you to be grateful?

5. **Say "Thank you."** Everyone likes to be thanked, and you'll feel more joy just for saying it, so say it often.

6. **Write thank-you notes.** I love writing thank-yous after hearing a great lesson at church or having a heartfelt moment with a friend. It's also wonderful to send notes "just because"—especially to those who have been there for you through your breakup.

7. **Text your loved ones a message of thanks.** "Thanks for your advice yesterday." "I am so grateful to have you in my life." Simple. Effective.

8. **Do the Three Blessings exercise.** At the dinner table or before bed, share three blessings that you and your loved ones experienced that day. This is also great when you have a bad day; after talking about the "bad" stuff or writing about it in your journal, you must list three blessings. Finally, this is a great exercise for kids, too.

9. **Acknowledge one ungrateful thought per day and replace it with a grateful one.** If you catch yourself thinking, "My ex is so selfish!" try replacing it with, "I am grateful I'm in a healthy place in my life and that I don't need to focus on what my ex does anymore." Using the techniques you learned in chapters 13 through 17, question and alter your thoughts. This gives you the power to bring in more gratitude and change your life—one ungrateful thought at a time.

Bottom Line...

- Don't wait to *feel* grateful; instead, *practice* gratitude.

- Practicing gratitude is key to living a life that flourishes.

Tool: Start a Gratitude Practice

♥ Read through the list of gratitude practice ideas above, and select one or two to try, or develop your own way to practice gratitude. Then get started being grateful. No excuses. Start today!

41 Discover meaning and purpose.

The meaning of life is to find your gift.
The purpose of life is to give it away.

—Anonymous

What Is Your Purpose?

What were you, and you alone, put on this earth to do? We all have one, you know: a purpose. And all life missions and purposes, in some way or another, revolve around love. No matter how old or young or tired or busy or uncertain—or single—you are, you have great work to do, my friend.

Have you felt the essence of what you were created to do? If not, what is standing in your way? Is it a lack of desire? Is it fear that your breakup has quashed your life's purpose? Whatever is holding you back, hear this: you will never feel at home until you discover, uncover, or recover your divine purpose and make it the focus of your life.

Purpose, Meaning, and Love

It's impossible to discover your life's purpose without first discovering meaning in your life. When a significant relationship ends, it can take the meaning from life along with it. We've lost love, and it feels like we'll never get it back again. Yet, as we seek to rediscover meaning, to infuse each day with purpose, we find that love is never lost but only transformed. We need only to seek in order to find love in our lives again. Love is what gives meaning to life—love of ourselves, love of others, love of what it is we were put on Earth to do—and meaning gives life purpose.

Listen Through the Passion to the Meaning

When we're talking about meaning and purpose, we're not just talking about living passionately. Though I'm definitely a fan of passion, there's a difference between passion's rush of excitement that gets you out of bed each day and meaning's deeper connection to something greater than yourself—whether you're in or out of bed. Your job is to listen *through* the passion for the meaning, then passionately infuse meaning—and love—into everything you do.

A life of meaning means we have a deeper connection to something greater than ourselves. So, what is meaningful to you? What values do you hold most dear? Family? Faith? Compassion? As we regularly check in on what matters most and make sure that we are living accordingly, we begin to experience a more meaningful life. We begin to sense our life's purpose.

Discover Your Life's Purpose

What *is* your life's purpose? It's a big question, I know. I could easily write a whole book about it (and someday probably will). Fulfilling your purpose is essential to a life of love, joy, and flourishing, but you can't fulfill your purpose until you realize what it is. Here are three recommendations to get you started:

1. **Pay attention to those activities, people, events, and experiences that light you up,** that make you feel passionate and excited about life. These are clues to what your purpose is all about.

2. **Your life's purpose doesn't have to be something "big";** in fact, usually it's not. Instead, purpose is about living even the small moments of life with great meaning.

3. **Discover your purpose day by day.** What gives your life meaning and purpose? If you're not sure yet, good for you. You get to discover it! Ask the following questions daily:

   - What matters most to me?

   - What gets me out of bed each day?

   - What do I feel most "at home" doing?

   - What are my strengths? What do these tell me about my purpose?

   - If I have a sense of my purpose, am I actively seeking to engage in it? If not, what is standing in my way?

Bottom Line...

- You can rediscover meaning after your breakup, and when you do you will be on the way to a flourishing life.

- You have a divine purpose—yes, *you*. Seek it and you shall find it.

Tool: Discover Daily Meaning and Uncover Your Life's Purpose

❤ What are your values? Do you value family, faith, honesty, courage, independence, hard work, integrity, or all of these? In your journal, list your core values. List as many things as you'd like. Focus on these things daily to bring more meaning to your life.

♥ Do the Mission Possible exercise. Create a growing list of all the things you enjoy. Include personality traits as well as talents, skills, hobbies, and those things that others seem to enjoy most about you. Mindfully examine this list, searching for themes. Are there one or two overarching themes of your life, such as teaching, caretaking, or adventure? These are part of your life's mission and purpose.

42 Live with vision.

The only thing worse than being blind
is having sight but no vision.

—Helen Keller

When you look at your future now, after your breakup, what do you see? Do you still cling to negative thoughts, worries, and fears that cloud your vision? Or are you finally experiencing clarity about who you are and what you're here to do? It's one thing to think, My *future has great potential*; it's another to actually see and live it.

What Is Vision?

Living with vision means creating a clear image of what you desire out of life, then remembering and working toward that image. Having a vision includes seeing the best possible outcomes for work, family, personal development, faith, and anything else that matters to you. It also includes seeing the best possible outcome for your future relationships.

How to Form Your Life's Vision

Your vision may involve a meaningful phrase, quote, or words to inspire you, or it may simply be closing your eyes and seeing those clear images over and again. I have found the following exercise particularly helpful in creating a life vision.

1. Review the exercises we've done, including your lists of values from the previous chapter, along with your To Be list and End of Life visualization from chapter 34. Circle those values, traits, and experiences that feel most important to you.

2. Group like things together—for instance, "compassion," "kindness," and "giving" could all be grouped under "love."

3. From the grouped list, choose three words that are most important to you. Write them down. For example, my three words are "faith, love, joy." These words encompass many other important aspects of my life, including family, contribution, spirituality, and growth. These three words express my life's vision. They're a simple, effective way to remind me of the meaning, purpose, and direction I desire my life to take each day. This exercise can give you the vision you are seeking, too.

Bottom Line...

- Envision the life you desire.

- Then remember your vision and work toward it each day. It really is that simple.

Tool: Create Your Vision

- ♥ Create your vision. Close your eyes. What do you envision for yourself, your family, friends, work, future, and, yes, your love life? Write it all down.

- ♥ Follow the steps in How to Form Your Life's Vision, above. How does this exercise make you feel? Does it help clarify your vision? Write about your experiences in your journal.

♥ Dream yourself to sleep. Instead of thinking of all your worries and stress as you drift off each night, imagine the best possible future for your loved ones and you. See it clearly in your mind. "Dreaming to sleep" not only helps you sleep more peacefully, it helps you wake ready to work, to see your vision come to reality.

43 Set a daily focus.

The very moment you wake up each morning...all your wishes and hopes for the day rush at you like wild animals. And the first job each morning consists in shoving them all back; in listening to that other voice, taking that other point of view, letting that other, larger, stronger, quieter life come flowing in.

—C. S. Lewis

Most of us wake up and go about our day without giving much thought to what we actually *want* for that day. We might *hope* for favorable circumstances, but are we actively seeking and implementing good things into our daily lives? If not, we can change this with one simple tool: setting a daily focus.

Why a Daily Focus?

It's essential to remind ourselves of our life's vision; what we focus on, we receive. We can't expect to get to that glorious future state of loving relationships, success, and joy if we don't work on it daily. A daily focus allows us to check in and bring more of what we desire into each day, instead of waiting passively for things to simply appear.

How to Select Your Daily Focus

Here are a few tips:

- **Get still.** When you've been going through a breakup, life may feel even busier than normal. It's even more vital to actively seek time and space away to meditate, pray, or ponder where you are and where you would like to be.

- **Ask yourself, "What do I most want, need, or desire from today?"** On dark days you may need to feel loved, to find understanding, or maybe just a little extra self-compassion. On brighter days, you may want to focus on feeling self-worth, acting with confidence, or smiling to bring a little more cheer to you and those around you.

- **Focus on creating *positive* emotions and experiences.** As we've already discussed, life isn't just about overcoming the negative stuff. We can also put more of the good stuff into each day—on purpose.

- **Stop focusing on what you *don't* want.** "I don't want to feel depressed," "I don't want to think of my ex today," "I do not want to be so negative!" Ironically, the more we focus on what we *don't* want, the more likely we are to get it.

- **Focus on what you *do* want.** Instead of saying, "I don't want to feel depressed," turn it around: "Today, I will create feelings of energy and peace." Instead of "I don't want to think of my ex today," say, "I will allow only healthy thoughts today." Instead of "I do not want to be so negative!" say, "I am seeking the good in each moment."

- **Seek the good.** When we actively seek, we can always find some good in every situation. Instead of waking up and thinking, "Ugh. Another day. I am so tired," seek the good— "I am grateful to be alive and in good health this morning." That tiny shift can make a huge difference in your day. That's what a daily focus is all about.

Bottom Line...

- A daily focus reminds us of our life's vision and keeps us on track.

- A daily focus helps us seek the good and bring more of what we desire into each day.

Tool: Set Your Daily Focus

♥ Set aside a few minutes of quiet time each morning. I do this as part of the time I designate for exercise, scripture, prayer, and meditation. First, repeat your vision to yourself. Then think about what is coming your way today, and open yourself up to the focus that will most help you. Some days my focus is, "Breathe. Just breathe." Other times it's more like, "I am peace. I am love. I am joy."

44 Choose to create the life you desire.

Between stimulus and response there is a space.
In that space is our power to choose our response.
In our response lies our growth and our freedom.

—Viktor Frankl

Too often we allow the thoughts and feelings of the past to rule our mind, heart, and even our spirit. As the clouds roll in, we submit, and, like Eeyore, mumble, "Well, it's going to rain, no chance of sun for me today," turning back to hide in our cold, dark cave. We fail to embrace our power to choose, to create what we want despite the weather—to grab an umbrella, a raincoat, and polka-dot rain boots, then head out to seek our good fortune. As Holocaust survivor and psychiatrist Viktor Frankl reminds us in the quote above, between feelings, thoughts, and behaviors, we have *choice*.

Desire, Believe, Create

How do we create the life we desire? The answer is simple: we choose to *desire*, and then we *create*. Creating is what gets us out of old habits and patterns that aren't working and onto a new and improved path. It is how we put our life's vision, purpose, and mission to use.

Now, don't you dare tell me, "I can't create my life. I'm not creative." Every one of us is blessed with the creativity we need to create the life we desire. The only thing that stands in our way is the need to believe in ourselves—then it's simply a matter of getting out there and doing the work of creation.

The Three Steps of Creation

It may seem difficult to do—"the work of creation"—and, certainly, it takes time and effort. But it becomes much simpler when you use the following three steps.

1. **See your current "reality."** Seeing means you remove the rose-colored glasses and take a good, hard look at the ups and downs, strengths and weaknesses, experiences and "problems" that make up your current life. We've been working on "seeing" reality throughout this book, so you should be getting the hang of it by now. Only once you have seen the current reality can you begin to envision a new one.

2. **Desire a different reality.** Some people have trouble with this task because they think it's "selfish" to desire. Believe me, it's not. I'm talking about knowing what lies in your heart and embracing it; reaching out and working for your dreams; creating your self and your life into the best they can be. What do *you* desire?

3. **Create what you desire.** What must be done to achieve that vision, that end result you dream about? Setting a daily focus can help. You can also set daily goals to shape your life into what you desire. Choose one small thing you can create today and begin there. Then create the next step. And the next. If you desire more love, create more love in your life by being more loving. If you desire more peace, reach out in peace today. Bit by bit, your creations become your reality, and your reality will be the life you have always desired.

Tips for Creating the Life You Desire

Still unsure exactly *how* to create the life you desire? The following suggestions can be a big help:

- **Let your desires take hold.** What you *do* with them will come later; for now, just let yourself desire.

- **Your desires are uniquely yours.** Let go of the urge to look around and compare yourself to others. Only *you* know the true path for your life.

- **Creating the life you desire isn't about adding more to-dos.** Instead, it's about working on that To Be list we created in chapter 34. As you focus on who you want to be, the life you desire will take form.

- **Let go of your preconceived ideas of what's possible.** Suspend your current concept of reality, of what you can or cannot do or become. Who's to say what's possible for you?

Bottom Line...

- Only you can choose to create the life you desire.

- If you persistently follow the Three Steps of Creation, in time, you *will* create the life you desire. (And if the first time doesn't work, well, you can continually restart the process—see, desire, and create—until your life becomes what you envision it to be!)

Tool: Desire and Create

♥ Are you able to discern the desires of your heart? If so, make a list of your current desires. If you struggle with desire, start dreaming. As we've done before, let yourself imagine all kinds of possibilities for your life. Imagine where you might go, what you might do, and, especially, who you might become. There is no right or wrong. Let go and dream away.

♥ Use the Three Steps of Creation given in this chapter, to begin to create the life you desire, today.

45 The "good" life isn't necessarily the best life.

The good life is a process, not a state of being.
It is a direction, not a destination.

—Carl Rogers

After a breakup, we want to return to a "good" life, and the sooner the better. But are we selling ourselves short if we do? Positive psychology has identified three types of "lives," or ways to happiness: the Pleasant Life, the Engaged Life, and the Meaningful Life. Research shows that the happiest people are those who pursue all three—the pleasant, the engaging, and the meaningful (Duckworth, Steen, and Seligman, 2005).

Living the Pleasant Life

Imagine a beautiful spring day. The sun is out, the birds are chirping, and you are lying in a hammock taking it all in. Life is going well. You feel happy. This is what positive psychology calls the Pleasant Life.

The Pleasant Life is filled with positive emotion—like happiness, gratitude, satisfaction, and love—about the past, present, and future. It is also a life filled with pleasure—such as lying in that hammock, or doing whatever sounds fun in the moment. It is a life of hope and love. Yet, is it the best life? Hmm...

Living the Engaged Life

The Engaged Life includes feeling positive emotions and experiencing pleasure, like the Pleasant Life, but it goes further, including using your strengths to actively participate in life. People living the Engaged Life understand their signature strengths—their core values and abilities—and they use them to bring happiness to themselves and others. This gives them a greater sense of fulfillment than the Pleasant Life can offer. It may be more work, but that work holds the key to greater well-being and happiness.

Living the Meaningful Life

If we want the highest levels of satisfaction and flourishing, however, it's the Meaningful Life we should seek. The Meaningful Life includes the positive emotion and pleasure of the Pleasant Life and the strengths-based commitment of the Engaged Life, but it goes a step further. This is a life of meaning and purpose. It is a life devoted to serving others, and to being an active part of meaningful institutions like family, community, and faith. Think of those who, after suffering a great loss, go on to form a charity or foundation that helps others through a similar loss; or those who, despite their own hardships, seek to serve and uplift those around them. People like this are living the Meaningful Life. They work hard to be part of the greater whole, and the payoff is a life of flourishing—a life of love and joy, no matter what hardships may come.

What Kind of Life Will You Live?

So, what will it be for you? Will you choose to pursue the positive emotion and pleasure of a Pleasant Life? Will you seek engagement with your strengths to enjoy even greater happiness? Or are you willing to go for it and seek the Meaningful Life? The choice is yours.

Bottom Line...

- Positive psychology identifies three types of "lives": the Pleasant Life, the Engaged Life, and the Meaningful Life.

- It's up to you which life you pursue, but the Meaningful Life is associated with the highest levels of happiness.

Tool: Choose a Life to Live

♥ Revisit your Flourishing assessment from chapter 38 and your list of desires from chapter 44. Ask yourself, "Which type of life am I currently living?" "Which do I *desire* to live?" Are you willing to work for a Pleasant, Engaged, or Meaningful Life? If not, what's standing in your way? If so, what will it take to get you there? Write your responses in your journal.

46 Develop your mission statement.

Your purpose in life is to find your purpose
and give your whole heart and soul to it.

—Buddha (attributed)

You have your To Be list. You're discovering your purpose. You have a meaning and a vision for your life. Now, it's time to bring all that together into one concise, focused statement—your mission statement.

Why a Mission Statement?

Mission statements bring what you desire for the future into focus in the present. They outline what you are seeking and the steps you're taking to get there. A well-developed mission statement can keep you on the path of overcoming, becoming, and flourishing. It can help you break through whatever barriers come your way and reach your highest potential.

How to Develop a Mission Statement

Once we understand why we want to develop a mission statement, the next logical question is "How?" The following three steps can get you started:

1. **Review.** Pull out your journal and write down your vision. Revisit past exercises and remind yourself of who you are and who you're working to become. Think about the people in your life—your family, friends, community, and, yes, intimate relationships. What do you envision for these? Do you envision loving and being loved again? Write it all down.

2. **Brainstorm.** Based on the things you envision and have already discovered about yourself, brainstorm sentences for your mission statement. Write as many as you'd like.

3. **Refine.** Your ultimate goal is to boil it down to three to five sentences. Continue refining the words until they best fit the life you envision, until your statement most feels like the mission you're here to perform.

A Few Things to Keep in Mind

- It can often take months, or even years, to settle on a mission statement that feels right and true to you. Be patient and keep working on it.

- Make sure to *remember* your mission statement. There's no point in writing it if you don't remember to do what it says. Type it up and post it, set it as a screen saver, or write it in the front of your journal so you can refer to it often.

- As life's circumstances change, you will change, and that means your life's vision and how you plan to get there will change, too. Feel free to alter and adapt your mission statement to reflect where you are at each stage of life.

Bottom Line...

- Bring your life's vision, purpose, meaning, and goals in line with a written mission statement.

- A mission statement may take time and effort, but the payoff—living a life of meaning and purpose—is worth it.

Tool: Create Your Mission Statement

♥ Use the suggestions above to create your mission statement. Review past exercises, brainstorm, and keep refining until it's just right.

47 Learn to be an optimist!

A pessimist sees the difficulty in every opportunity;
an optimist sees the opportunity in every difficulty.

—Winston Churchill

It's easy to become pessimistic about yourself, life, and love after a breakup. We've worked to overcome the pessimistic thoughts, but let me ask you this, "Are you a pessimist or an optimist?" I used to say I was a "realist," but isn't that just another word for "optimistic pessimist?" Then, one day, I started studying optimism and realized that I was a lot more optimistic than I'd believed. I also learned that it doesn't matter whether you're an optimist by nature or not: optimism can be learned.

The Power of Optimism

Research shows that learning how to be more optimistic decreases symptoms of depression, increases one's sense of power in life, and is linked with higher levels of self-esteem and self-efficacy (Seligman 1990). Even the most pessimistic among us can benefit from learning a little optimism. Optimism is one of those traits, like gratitude, that can be developed and strengthened.

Learning Optimism

So how can you become an optimist? Here are a few suggestions:

- **Listen to what you tell yourself throughout each day.** Use your Thought Records, and be honest—are you making pessimistic comments all the time? Or are you optimistically facing challenges?

- **If you notice pessimistic thinking popping up, stop and replace it with the optimistic perspective.** When my good friend Erika was going through a difficult divorce, I was inspired by her optimism. Sure, she had pessimistic thoughts like, "I can't believe this is happening to me," and "I won't be able to handle four kids on my own!" But she learned to hear herself and turn it around: "I can do this. I know something great is out there waiting for my kids and me." A few years later, she is happily remarried, on friendly terms with her ex, and her kids are doing well. Having optimism as your companion is so much better than the alternative.

- **When you see no optimistic alternatives, seek them out.** Ask yourself, "If there *were* an optimistic view of this situation, what might it be?" Sometimes simply posing the question can turn things around.

- **If you hear your pessimistic beliefs creeping in after you've already turned them around, distract yourself.** Healthy distraction—going for a walk, watching TV, working on a project—can be a great tool to keep optimism flowing.

Bottom Line...

- Optimism can be learned and strengthened.

- Practice optimism and you'll feel healthier, happier, and more powerful in your life.

Tool: Practice Optimism

♥ Think of an optimistic mantra for your daily focus (see chapter 43). Try something like, "I am in the best possible circumstances for my optimal learning and growth."

♥ When faced with a stressful situation or pessimistic people, try to shine the optimistic light. If people are complaining because of a long line, smile and start a positive conversation. If your family is being pessimistic about your breakup, repeat, "I know this is going to work out for the best."

48 *Let* yourself shine!

**She not only saw a light at the end of the tunnel.
She became that light for others.**

—Anonymous

I love the quote above, from a card my mother-in-law gave me during one of my darkest times. It gave me hope that one day I would shine—not only for myself but for others. After all you've been through it would be easy to hide away, but you've seen that light at the end of the tunnel by now, haven't you? Can you become that light for others? We are not meant to dull ourselves; we are meant to shine.

How Do You Shine?

When I say "shine," I mean let the best parts of you—your strengths, your talents—proudly show. Don't hide them under a bushel; be a candle on a hill. We've worked to help you embrace your worth, to feel unwavering self-esteem, and learn to love and be loved again. What good are these things, however, if you don't put them into practice, if you don't let them show?

Some shine when they are leading; others shine when supporting. Some shine when working with children; others shine musically, artistically, or athletically. Some shine by being joyful, friendly, or funny; others by being a beacon of hope, goodwill, or love. In chapter 28 we began discovering your strengths. Now it's time to embrace those strengths, to use them to benefit not only you but those around you.

Let Yourself Shine

The word *let* is italicized for a reason. Only you can *let* yourself shine. Only you can get out there and show the world what you've got. Only you can choose to use the gifts that you have been given to bring a little light to your life and the lives around you. That's the result of shining. It lights you up. It lights up the world. And, in shining, we often stumble upon our greatest opportunities—whether it be a self-development opportunity, a work opportunity, or, yes, even a shiny, new love opportunity.

Bottom Line...

- We aren't meant to hide who we are; we are made to shine.

- Letting yourself shine is one of the most love-filled things we can do.

Tool: Get Out There and Shine!

- ♥ What does "shining" look like for you? In what ways can you envision being a "light" for others? Revisit your Strengths list (chapter 28), your life's vision (chapter 42), and Mission Statement (chapter 46). What do you have to offer to the world? Write about it in your journal.

- ♥ Engage in those activities that allow your light to shine! Choose one quality or talent you have to offer, then actively seek to let it shine.

49 Live the Golden Rule.

The most miserable people I know are those who are obsessed with themselves; the happiest people I know are those who lose themselves in the service of others.

—Gordon B. Hinckley

You know the Golden Rule, right? "Do unto others as you'd have them do unto you?" Well, now that you're feeling more "golden," it's time to make sure you're treating others in a similar way. Focusing on loving and serving others is one of the best ways to continue to build unwavering self-esteem, to love and be loved, and to keep that golden feeling going strong.

Self-Love Precedes Other-Love

It's impossible to truly love others until you love yourself. You can't give what you don't already have. Hopefully, you're practicing self-love now. And if you are, you're ready to apply that same love to others in your life. It is in loving and serving others that we discover true meaning and purpose; it is through loving that we develop healthy relationships. We need other people. We need to love and be loved in return, and when we allow this cycle to be complete, we find greater love, connection, and joy.

How to Practice the Golden Rule

The Golden Rule isn't about becoming a doormat. It's about loving and serving others. One of the surest signs that we are flourishing in self-esteem is that we treat ourselves, and others, with respect, that we obey the Golden Rule. Here's how, in a few steps:

1. **Assess how well you're doing with the Golden Rule so far.** Have you felt loving toward your family? Toward friends and coworkers? Your ex? Have you sought opportunities to treat them kindly, show them love, and serve when they're in need? If you find your love blocked for any of these people, don't worry. Seeing is the first step. It also means you have some work to do.

2. **Choose one person you've had a hard time loving and do something kind for him or her today.** It might be as simple as a smile or a kind word. It might be an act of service, a listening ear, or a shoulder on which to cry. Whatever it may be, reach out in love, on purpose, today.

3. **Branch out to others, including strangers.** The more you practice purposefully living the Golden Rule, the easier it will become to extend it to others, including more-difficult friends and family, and, yes, even strangers. Strangers are actually a great source to practice. Think about how you wish others would treat you, then, when you're out and about, extend others that same courtesy.

4. **Practice the Golden Rule with your ex.** Especially if you've had a messy breakup or divorce, it can feel like you never want to extend kindness his way at all. This is not healthy, though. You don't have to become friends again, or even have a relationship, but as we discussed in chapter 36, it only hurts you if you fail to forgive. Instead, you can choose to give him the respect you wish he had given you, expecting nothing in return but a deeper sense of inner peace.

5. **Practice service.** Numerous studies show the benefits of altruistic service (Post 2005). You might volunteer at a hospital, make someone dinner, babysit for a friend, or sit with someone in need and listen. Serving others is one of the best ways to use your talents, feel self-worth, and develop deeper, lasting joy.

Bottom Line...

- The Golden Rule reminds us to extend to others the same love and respect we've developed for ourselves.

- Following the Golden Rule is the gateway to giving and receiving greater love in our lives.

Tool: Live the Golden Rule

- ❤ Practice loving others more fully using the tips above. This includes your family, friends, and, yes, your ex. When you're in public, look for ways to treat others as you would like to be treated, or even better. When with family or friends, seek opportunities to serve.

- ❤ Volunteer for a worthy cause. Serving others is an important part of flourishing.

50 Engage in healthy, loving relationships.

I've been fighting to be who I am all my life.
What's the point of being who I am, if I can't have
the person who was worth all the fighting for?

—Stephanie Lennox

Stop for a moment and catch your breath. You've been working so hard and have come so far. You have learned to ditch unwanted thoughts, to overcome anger, blame, and fear. You have uncovered the real you and learned to embrace your shadow and your potential. You have implemented positive practices like gratitude and optimism. But what is the point of all this work if you don't have healthy relationships—people in your life who see and love the real you, too?

You've discovered your worth on your own. You've done that work for *you*. You are now in the perfect position to seek healthy, loving, even *new* relationships.

Getting Back Out There

When I say it's time to seek new, healthy relationships, I'm not saying you need to get out there and start dating or enter into an intimate relationship—yet. That may be your goal at this point; you may have already started on that goal. Or you may feel completely unready to take on dating—indefinitely. Only you will know if and when you are ready for a new intimate relationship.

What I am saying is, if you've done the work in this book, then you're ready to share it with others. Not just *any* "others"—people who matter to you, people to whom *you* matter.

Where to Start

You may want to start with people you already know—perhaps those in your support system. Focus on strengthening those relationships you most value. Then branch out. Perhaps you have a coworker you'd like to get to know better, or a friend of a friend with whom you think you'd click.

Create new relationships that allow both of you to feel valued, uplifted, and authentic. Relationships like these are a keystone of a flourishing life. Creating healthy, loving relationships will not only reinforce your newfound sense of unwavering self-esteem, it will increase it. It will also, hopefully, help you feel ready for a healthy *romantic* relationship when the right person comes along.

A few things to keep in mind:

- **Seek relationships with people who inspire you to be your best.** Don't settle for relationships that bring you down. Don't even settle for relationships that keep you where you are. Look for people who uplift, motivate, and inspire you. Then, bring out the best in them, too.

- **Remember your boundaries and feel free to use them**. Boundaries are what *make* a healthy relationship. Without them, we'd lose ourselves in other people. Allow yourself to set up boundaries that protect you and others while still letting the love in.

- **Remember your values, purpose, and vision.** Healthy relationships are a major part of life values, purpose, and vision. If your relationships do not fit easily and clearly with these things, you may want to reconsider.

- **Invite love in.** Healthy relationships involve two things: loving and letting love in. I know you've been hurt before, but dare to open up your heart now. Love fully; invite love fully in.

Bottom Line...

- It's time to share your newfound sense of self with others who *matter*—and to whom you matter as well.

- Creating new, healthy, loving relationships reinforces and even increases self-esteem. They are a keystone of a flourishing life.

Tool: How to Know If a Relationship Is Healthy

♥ Ask yourself, "Can I be the real me in this relationship?" If so, it's probably healthy. If not, ask, "What is holding me back? Can I change that?" If the answer is "No, I can't change what prevents me from being the real me," the relationship is not healthy. If the answer is "yes," then start changing.

51 Let the light and love in.

The only whole heart is a broken one
because it lets the light in.

—David J. Wolpe

We're nearing the end of our journey together. I hope you've learned some valuable lessons and received some helpful tools. Hopefully, you have room for another lesson, one I believe is most important. That lesson is this: let the light and love in.

Don't Block the Light

When I say, "Let the light in," I mean let in life's lessons. Let in the beauty of the world. Let in the peaceful moments and joyful experiences. Let yourself flourish.

After you've been through a breakup, divorce, or any life trauma or challenge, it's easy to feel discouraged. It's easy to doubt the beauty, peace, and joy of the world. Yet, as we've worked through this book together, you have undoubtedly experienced some of that beauty, peace, and joy—in *you*. As long as it is in you, it can be found anywhere. All you have to do is look. Don't block the light, the wisdom, the spirituality, the hope, the goodness waiting for you.

Don't Block the Love

When I say, "Let love in," I mean open up your heart and keep it open. It's easy to let it close, especially when we've been hurt. We fear opening and being hurt again. By now, though, you can see all you have to offer when you open and share your heart, *and* all you have to lose if you close and lock it up.

Open. Open again. And again. And again. Keep opening your heart to love. It doesn't have to come from a romantic partner (though if it does, more power to you); just make sure you don't miss the love that is all around. From yourself. From your family. From your kids. From your support system and friends. From God.

And, if romantic love *is* on your horizon, this time, you know what you want. You know what you *do not* want. Most importantly, you know who you are, and you will not let yourself settle for anything less than the healthy, loving relationship you deserve.

That's the final lesson. Let. Love. In.

Bottom Line...

- Let the light—learning, wisdom, growth—in.

- Let the love—gentleness, value, appreciation, goodness—in, too.

Tool: Look for Love

- ♥ In nature, in friends, in family, in a book, in new romantic interests, in fulfilling your life's mission—look for love. Life is full of love. Seek it. Feel it. Let it in.

52 It only gets better from here.

> It doesn't matter where you are, you are nowhere compared to where you can go.
>
> **—Bob Proctor**

Just because you feel whole and healthy now doesn't mean you won't ever feel broken again. Unfortunately, you will. Unfortunately, we all do. Discovering self-worth and feeling self-esteem are lifelong processes.

But now, you know how to overcome. You know how to become. You know how to flourish. You need never feel as broken as you did when we started. Never again! Just revisit these tools anytime you or your relationships need a little rebuilding.

Hard times come and go, but your sense of self-worth, your experience of self-esteem, and a life of purpose, joy, and *love* can continue to grow for as long as you nurture it.

Bottom Line...

- Trust me when I say: It only gets better from here.

Tool: Congratulations, You've Done It!

♥ Give yourself a hug. Ask someone you love to hug you. You've made it to the end. You've worked hard. You deserve it.

Acknowledgments

First, to Wendy Millstine: this book would not be without you. I wasn't so sure I was the best person to write it, but you believed in me, and now I can see how right you were. I am deeply grateful you found me, and thank you for your endless encouragement and support.

To Jess Beebe and the editing team at New Harbinger: thank you. Your insights and feedback guided my writing and inspired me. To Becky Bagley, for stepping in and helping me finish this book when I was suddenly shoved back into "brokenness." You are and ever shall remain "the bomb." To Marisa Solís, my copy editor, can I just say, "Wow"? You make me look good. Thank you! Finally, to Rachel Rogers, Katie Parr, and everyone at New Harbinger who had a hand in publishing and marketing this book: I couldn't have done it without such a sharp team bringing the magic! And to Sue Patton Thoele, not only for drafting a beautiful foreword but for taking an interest in me and in my work. Your words of wisdom and compassion have comforted and moved me.

Finally, I thank my family—my children Braxton, Tre, Colton, Brody, Kennedy, and Sydney—for understanding and helping out when "Mom has to write today—again," and for believing in me as an author and mother. Oh, and for countless hugs—you know how I love my hugs! And to my dear husband, OJ, I dedicate this book. You told me to "Go for it" and then exercised great patience. Thank you for encouraging me to fulfill my life's purpose, and for your constant willingness to work at this crazy thing called marriage—for never giving up on us. It's quite a ride!

References

American Psychological Association. 2013. "Marriage and Divorce." Accessed July 25. http://www.apa.org/topics/divorce/.

Beck, A. T. 1976. *Cognitive Therapy and the Emotional Disorders*. New York: International Universities Press.

Branden, N. 1995. *The Six Pillars of Self-Esteem: The Definitive Work on Self-Esteem by the Leading Pioneer in the Field*. New York: Bantam Books.

Brown, B. 2012. *Daring Greatly: How the Courage to Be Vulnerable Transforms the Way We Live, Love, Parent, and Lead*. New York: Gotham Books.

Brown, K. W., and R. M. Ryan. 2003. "The Benefits of Being Present: Mindfulness and Its Role in Psychological Well-Being." *Journal of Personality and Social Psychology* 84: 822–48.

Divorce Statistics. 2013. "Divorce Statistics and Divorce Rate in the USA." Accessed August 10. http://www.divorcestatistics.info/divorce -statistics-and-divorce-rate-in-the-usa.html.

Duckworth, A. L., T. A. Steen, and M. E. Seligman. 2005. "Positive Psychology in Clinical Practice." *Annual Review of Clinical Psychology* 1: 629–51.

Emmons, R. A. 2007. *Thanks! How the New Science of Gratitude Can Make You Happier.* New York: Houghton Mifflin Company.

Emmons, R. A., and C. M. Shelton. 2002. "Gratitude and the Science of Positive Psychology." In *Handbook of Positive Psychology*, edited by C. R. Snyder and S. J. Lopez. Oxford: Oxford University Press.

Fredrickson, B. L., and M. F. Losada. 2005. "Positive Affect and Complex Dynamics of Human Flourishing." *American Psychologist* 60: 678–686.

Hibbert, C. 2013. *This Is How We Grow: A Psychologist's Memoir of Loss, Motherhood, and Discovering Self-Worth and Joy, One Season at a Time.* Flagstaff, AZ: Oracle Folio Books.

Kabat-Zinn, J. 2012. *Mindfulness for Beginners: Reclaiming the Present Moment—and Your Life.* Boulder, CO: Sounds True Inc.

Kübler-Ross, E., and D. Kessler. 2005. *On Grief and Grieving: Finding the Meaning of Grief Through the Five Stages of Loss.* New York: Schribner.

Neff, K. 2011. *Self-Compassion: Stop Beating Yourself Up and Leave Insecurity Behind.* New York: William Morrow/HarperCollins.

Post, S. 2005. "Altruism, Happiness, and Health: It's Good to Be Good." *International Journal of Behavioral Medicine* 12 2: 66–77.

Psychology Today. 2013. "Psych Basics: Self-Esteem." Accessed February 22. http://www.psychologytoday.com/basics/self-esteem.

Rando, T. A. 1984. *Grief, Dying, and Death: Clinical Interventions for Caregivers.* Champaign, IL: Research Press Co.

Seligman, M. 1990. *Learned Optimism: How to Change Your Mind and Your Life.* New York: Vintage Books.

Seligman, M. 2009. "Positive Psychology." *Evolution of Psychology Conference.* Lecture conducted in Anaheim, CA. December.

Seligman, M., T. A. Steen, N. Park, and C. Peterson. 2005. "Positive Psychology Progress: Empirical Validation of Interventions." *American Psychologist* July–August: 410–421.

Worden, W. 2008. *Grief Counseling and Grief Therapy: A Handbook for the Mental Health Practitioner.* Fourth edition. New York: Springer Publishing Co.

Christina G. Hibbert, PsyD, is a clinical psychologist and expert on women's mental health, grief, motherhood, postpartum health, parenting, self-esteem, and personal growth. She is author of the IPPY Award-winning memoir *This is How We Grow,* and co-producer of the internationally-sold DVD *Postpartum Couples.* Hibbert is founder of the Arizona Postpartum Wellness Coalition, a non-profit organization, and is a popular and dynamic speaker. She lives in the mountains of Flagstaff, AZ with her husband and six children. Learn more about Hibbert, her blog, speaking, and books at www .drchristinahibbert.com.

Foreword writer **Sue Patton Thoele** is a psychotherapist, former hospice chaplain, and bereavement group leader. She is author of several books, including *The Courage to Be Yourself.*